Praise for Becoming

"*Becoming Like Creoles* recognizes how intersectionality and cultural understandings open our eyes to a better reality. The authors sound a prophetic call to confront injustice. As personal narratives weave into biblical and theological understandings of justice, this profoundly important and insightful book challenges us to rethink and reimagine a just world."
—GRACE JI-SUN KIM, associate professor of theology at Earlham School of Religion and the author or editor of sixteen books, including *Embracing the Other*

"For this South African, more and more aware of the essential creoleness of our own society locked in battle with our racist, separatist, disconnected past, this book is a revelation and an invitation to think anew about things that were always so obvious yet so elusive. The personal stories strengthen rather than distract from the core argument and rhythm of this wonderful book, brimming over with fresh, provocative, and delightful insights. This book will change hearts and minds."
—ALLAN AUBREY BOESAK, South African Black liberation theologian and human rights activist

"DeYoung's writing never fails to invigorate my theological imagination—and *Becoming Like Creoles* is no exception! A wise collaboration between DeYoung and powerhouse thinker-leaders Jacqueline J. Lewis, Micky ScottBey Jones, Robyn Afrik, Sarah Thompson Nahar, Sindy Morales Garcia, and 'Iwalani Ka'ai, this book plunged me deeper into the word creole, uncovering the many ways in which it can expand and guide my own personal transformation as well the community transformation for which I advocate. I definitely plan to use it both personally and professionally, and I hope you will too!"
—CHRISTENA CLEVELAND, activist, public theologian, and director of the Center for Justice and Renewal

"*Becoming Like Creoles* presents a uniquely biblical model for our inter-racial/intercultural future that offers new life for both the oppressed and oppressor in a rehumanized community. In this important work, DeYoung masterfully blends six contemporary women of color in the narrative, so as to amplify their voices rather than appropriate them. Perhaps the most important question the book answers is whether whites can be recultured and rehumanized. The answer to this question brought me joy and hope for a reconciled future."
—RANDY WOODLEY, Indigenous speaker and author of *Shalom and the Community of Creation: An Indigenous Vision*

Becoming Like Creoles

Becoming Like Creoles

*Living and Leading at the Intersections of Injustice,
Culture, and Religion*

CURTISS PAUL DEYOUNG, LEAD AUTHOR

CONTRIBUTING AUTHORS

JACQUELINE J. LEWIS,
MICKY SCOTTBEY JONES,
ROBYN AFRIK,
SARAH THOMPSON NAHAR,
SINDY MORALES GARCIA,
AND 'IWALANI KA'AI

FORTRESS PRESS
MINNEAPOLIS

BECOMING LIKE CREOLES
Living and Leading at the Intersections of Injustice, Culture, and Religion

Scripture quotations are from the New Revised Standard Version Bible © 1989 Division of Christian Education of the National Council of the Churches of Christ in the United States of America. Used by permission.

Cover image: "Circle of Friends" by Alvin Clayton
Cover design: Laurie Ingram

Print ISBN: 978-1-5064-5556-3
eBook ISBN: 978-1-5064-5557-0

The paper used in this publication meets the minimum requirements of American National Standard for Information Sciences — Permanence of Paper for Printed Library Materials, ANSI Z329.48-1984.

Manufactured in the U.S.A.

Contents

Prelude

CURTISS PAUL DEYOUNG

In June 2008, I was invited by Sorbonne-educated sociologist Jean-Claude Girondin to speak in Paris, France, at a symposium called "Une Marche aux côtés de Martin Luther King" honoring the fortieth anniversary of King's death.[1] The conference was organized to provide a forum for discussing race and religion in a nation that rarely spoke of either. I was the only non-French speaker invited to lecture. The other presenters were scholars of Dr. King from the French-speaking world.[2] I participated in an expanded program on King in November 2008 that was offered at multiple locations on the Isle of Guadeloupe, a department of France in the Caribbean where citizens are primarily of African descent—and the birthplace of Dr. Girondin.[3] Once again I was the only non–French-language speaker. The conference organizers in Guadeloupe arranged for a group of English language teachers to serve as my translators—translating my English into French for the listening audience, and the French of the other lecturers into English for my edification.

In addition to engaging in a much more rigorous discussion of racism while in Guadeloupe, I was also introduced to the Creole language and culture of the island. Marquise Armand, one of the assigned English translators who specializes in the Creole language, began to share with me the nuanced differences in expression that led a person from Guadeloupe to speak in Creole or French, or a mix of both. During a church service where Marquise was translating for me, I noticed a parishioner began praying in French and then switched to Creole. Marquise explained to me that the woman used French to describe the majesty of God, but Creole was used to express the deep heart issues in her life.

In preparation for the symposium on Martin Luther King Jr. in Guadeloupe, I discovered the book *Éloge de la Créolité / In Praise of Creoleness* by French Caribbean authors Jean Bernabé, Patrick Chamoiseau, and Raphaël Confiant. The book begins with the exclamation, "Neither Europeans, nor Africans, nor Asians, we proclaim ourselves to be Creoles."[4] The New Testament descriptions of the first-century church sound much like the sentiments expressed by the authors of *Éloge de la Créolité / In Praise of Creoleness*. The apostle Paul wrote, "There is neither Jew nor Gentile, neither slave nor free, nor is there male and female, for you are all one in Christ Jesus" (Gal 3:28 NIV). As I read *Éloge de la Créolité*, I was struck by the idea that Creoleness could offer a metaphor for the reconciling of humanity as celebrated in the first-century church. As I will argue in this book, beginning at Pentecost, a creolization-like process occurred, forming intercultural congregations in the context of Roman Empire colonization, oppression, and injustice. Unique among the many images used for discussing diversity, equity, and inclusion, Creoleness is formed within a history of racism, injustice, oppression, and colonization. Therefore, creolization offers a way of envisioning a future through the interplay between cultural diversity, injustice and oppression, power differentials, and intersectionality.

Since my visits to Guadeloupe in 2008 and again in 2011,[5] I have read many of the volumes written about the Creole cultures that have emerged in the French West Indies. But I remain most moved by the words of the three Martinique writers Jean Bernabé, Patrick Chamoiseau, and Raphaël Confiant. I am struck by the many relevant and refreshing insights that emerge in their book. *Éloge de la Créolité / In Praise of Creoleness* is the starting point for my premise that we must become like Creoles. I am limited by the fact that my readings on creolization have been English translations from French originals. Even the French language versions potentially obscure the full meaning of Creole language concepts. In the same way, I read the New Testament using English translations from the Greek originals, and the Greek versions may miss some of the nuances found in the original Aramaic oral tradition. I make no claim to be any kind of scholar of Creole language or culture. I borrow "Creole" for its metaphorical power. I draw upon the Creole that has emerged in the French West Indies—a specific formulation—rather than using a generic understanding. Other Creole cultures around the globe have formed differently. *Éloge de la Créolité* has been critiqued, and there has been further development in the conversation on creolization. I have familiarized myself with many of these discussions.

The goal of *Becoming Like Creoles: Living and Leading at the Intersections of Injustice, Culture, and Religion* is to identify and recommend creolization-like processes for congregations and faith leaders in the twenty-first century. The roots of these processes are in first-century congregations described in the New Testament, while the twenty-first century is a world that beckons us to declare, as do the *Éloge de la Créolité* authors, "Neither Europeans, nor Africans, nor Asians, we proclaim ourselves to be Creoles." Using biblical exposition in conversation with present-day Creole metaphors, cultural competency research, whiteness studies, interreligious peacemaking practices, and real-life narratives, *Becoming Like Creoles* seeks to awaken and prepare people of faith to live and lead in a world where injustice is real and cultural diversity is rapidly increasing. Emerging leaders in the faith community are often women and persons of color stuck in status quo, white-male models of leadership. Whites are struggling in a time of Black Lives Matter, immigrant and refugee rights, and the re-emergence of indigenous voices. This book hopes to equip folks to embrace a Creole-like process, becoming culturally competent and social-justice focused, whether they are emerging from a history of injustice or heirs of various forms of privilege or white supremacy.

In this writing task I am joined by six women as contributing authors who are persons of color or Indigenous (POCI). *Becoming Like Creoles* unfolds in four sections that bring together the conceptual and the illustrative. Do not let the mix of theological, theoretical, and experiential limit your engagement with the content of the book. These three dimensions are all necessary to achieve the foundational understandings, needed competencies, and required outcomes. The first section explains creolization concepts and its communal expression. Chapter 1 unpacks the Creole metaphor, presents the biblical church launched on the Day of Pentecost as a Creole-like community, and delineates lessons from the first-century church, so faith communities can authentically engage the realities of the twenty-first century. The story of the highly diverse Middle Collegiate Church in the East Village of New York City illustrates a modern-day Pentecost, Creole-like reality. This second chapter is written by Jacqueline J. Lewis, the current senior minister at Middle Collegiate Church. The second section focuses on how to develop leaders who exhibit Creole-like skills. Chapter 3 examines the five multicultural leaders in Antioch (Acts 13:1) in conversation with cultural competency literature. In chapter 4, five present-day, culturally competent, faith-inspired women—Micky ScottBey Jones, Robyn Afrik, Sarah Thompson Nahar, Sindy Morales Garcia, and 'Iwalani Ka'ai—tell their stories.

The third section examines the potential for whites and people of privilege to embrace creolization using Jesus's conversation with a woman at Jacob's Well in Samaria as a starting point. Chapter 5 continues the discussion of creolization and cultural competency, and adds whiteness studies. In chapter 6, the lead author applies this analysis to his own journey as a white male traversing diverse spaces. The final chapter moves this conversation of Creoleness into the realm of religious intersections. The story of Abraham's sons Ishmael and Isaac (representative of Islam, Judaism, and Christianity) joining together to bury their father at the cave of Machpelah becomes an image of interfaith competency. An examination of interreligious peacemaking literature and the journey of Eliyahu McLean and other leaders among the Jerusalem Peacemakers offers a contemporary look at the possibilities for interfaith competency.

Becoming Like Creoles is a public theology, a lived experience, and a leadership imperative that equips people for a social-justice struggle that is informed by intersectionality and cultural competence. This book is an invitation to a future that is knocking at the door and yet is already here—"a question to be lived!"[6]

Notes

1. Symposium: Une Marche aux côtés de Martin Luther King, sponsored by Agape France and the Protestant Federation of France, Reformed Church of the Oratory of the Louvre, Paris, France, June 14, 2008.

2. Serge Molla was among the French-speaking scholars of King who was lecturing. He has three books published in French on King. Because we met, he would later translate into French my book *Living Faith: How Faith Inspires Social Justice* (Minneapolis: Fortress, 2007) as *Mystiques en action: Trois modèles pour le XXIe siècle: Dietrich Bonhoeffer, Malcolm X, Aung San Suu Kyi* (Genève, Switzerland: Labor et fides, 2010).

3. Symposium: Une Marche aux côtés de Martin Luther King, sponsored by Agape France and the Protestant Federation of France, Les Abymes and Lamentin, Guadeloupe, November 18–21, 2008.

4. Jean Bernabé, Patrick Chamoiseau, and Raphaël Confiant, *Éloge de la Créoloité / In Praise of Creoleness, Édition Bilingue* (Paris: Gallimard, 1993), 75.

5. Symposium: Justice, Paix et Réconciliation: L'exemple de Martin Luther King, sponsored by Agape Media, Les Abymes and Lamentin, Guadeloupe, January 22–26, 2011.

6. Bernabé et al., *Éloge de la Créoloité*, 89.

1.

Day of Pentecost: Creolization in Colonization

CURTISS PAUL DEYOUNG

The second chapter of Acts begins with an event on the day of the Jewish feast of Shavout, called Pentecost by Diaspora Jews—fifty days following Passover. Galilean Jewish followers of Jesus, who had been waiting in Jerusalem for over a month after his death and resurrection (Acts 1:4), likely sequestered in an upper room, entered the streets of Jerusalem shouting in various languages that were not their mother tongue. People from Jewish enclaves on the continents of Asia, Africa, and Europe, who had immigrated to Jerusalem or were there for the Pentecost feast, heard these proclamations in the local dialect from their country of origin. Converts to Judaism from the capital city of Rome, as well as Cretans and Arabs, were also present, hearing Jesus's followers in their own languages. Given the feast-day throng, Roman Empire soldiers were likely on alert at the edges of the crowd, poised to exert measures of empire control if necessary, and even they were hearing in their own language (Acts 2:1–12).

The author of Acts also narrates other occasions when power was deconstructed through Pentecost-like events. On the day of Pentecost in Jerusalem, the Spirit created communities where second-class Galilean Jews and Diasporic Jews were thrust into leadership in a place that was the domain of established, Jerusalem-based priestly Jewish families (2:37–42). As the Spirit visited Samaria (8:4–25), an inclusive equality was created between Samaritans, who were marginalized in Jewish society, and Jews. Oppressed Jews gained equal status with ruling-class Romans when the Spirit came to the home of the Roman centurion Cornelius (10:1–48). The Spirit also moved outside these Roman-dominated communities to create a shared faith between an oppressed Jew and an

Ethiopian finance minister from Rome's equally powerful rival empire, ancient Nubia, ruled by Queen Candice (8:26–40). The faith communities that emerged from these encounters offered healing by restoring a sense of human dignity to marginalized oppressed groups, dismantling the power and privilege of their oppressors, and reconciling society's divisions.

First-century Pentecost preachers entered oppressed Jewish communities throughout the Roman Empire to establish embryonic congregations that were places of healing for oppressed and colonized Jews. Faith communities were developed with the expressed purpose of countering the harmful effects of colonialism, internalized oppression, and demeaned and diminished identities. The Roman Empire propagated the idea that Jews were "good for nothing but slavery."[1] Yet these Jewish Pentecost preachers witnessed that through embracing Jesus Christ, their damaged, enslaved, and colonized identities were healed and returned to their original design as created in the image of God. A colonially enforced identity could be swapped for a liberated identity in Jesus Christ (2 Cor 5:16–17).

As members of oppressed Jewish faith communities decolonized and reconciled, they then reached out to persons of power and privilege.[2] They considered the possibility that perhaps Romans who were members of the oppressing group and Greeks who benefited from Roman oppression could be liberated from beliefs in supremacy and ways of domination, so true reconciliation could occur. Many Romans and Greeks embraced this decolonizing and reconciliation process by replacing their loyalty to the empire with faith in Jesus. They refused to be defined by the privileges that go with power and position and joined faith communities with those who were oppressed.

Romans and Greeks entered small, Jewish, home-based congregations and reconciled, that is, socially exchanged, places with oppressed Jews.[3] In these intimate settings, familial bonds were formed. Romans and Greeks became identified with socially stigmatized Jews as they discarded privileged perspectives and positions. They were adopted by marginalized people—becoming family with Jews who were oppressed by Rome. Privileged Romans and Greeks were under the leadership of and mentored by oppressed Jews. Romans were worshiping and pledging allegiance to Jesus of Nazareth, who was crucified as an enemy of their empire. All this produced life-altering repercussions for Romans and Greeks in their lifestyle, social status, and identity in the Roman Empire. Therefore, the New Testament model of faith communities was one where an oppressed minority community welcomed people from the privileged, dominant culture into the local congregation.[4]

As the preachers of Pentecost moved out of Palestine into the Roman-dominated European and Asian continents, intercultural congregations emerged that were composed of colonized Jewish subjects of Rome living in community with and exercising leadership over Greeks and Romans from the dominant culture. Such congregations were found in Antioch (Acts 11:19–26), Cyprus (13:4–12), Pisidian Antioch (13:14–52), Iconium (14:1–5), Philippi (16:11–15), Thessalonica (17:1–9), Beroea (17:10–15), Corinth (18:1–18), Ephesus (18:19–21; 19:1–20:1), Rome (2:10; 28:14–30; see also Romans), and likely throughout the entire Roman Empire. First-century congregations created communities where cultures resonated, interacted, and blended with each other, where power dynamics were acknowledged and reversed, and relations—including those between women and men—could be made right.

In 1989, linguist Jean Bernabé, social worker Patrick Chamoiseau, and linguist Raphaël Confiant wrote *Éloge de la Créolité / In Praise of Creoleness*. They declared,

> Neither Europeans, nor Africans, nor Asians, we proclaim ourselves Creoles. This will be for us an interior attitude—better, a vigilance, or even better, a sort of mental envelope in the middle of which our world will be built in full consciousness of the outer world. These words we are communicating to you here do not stem from theory, nor do they stem from any learned principles. They are, rather, akin to testimony.[5]

The Creoleness that emerged in the French West Indies has been called "the purest example of the kind of cultural hybridization that occurs when different peoples are thrown together."[6] The arrival of the Spirit on the day of Pentecost and at the launch of congregations in the first century were Creole-like moments. The church, at its best, is a Creole-like movement.

A Creole-like community of thousands of intercultural, multilingual Jews emerged in Jerusalem, in the heart of the Roman-occupied Palestinian territories. The day of Pentecost placed a Creole imprint upon the church from its inception. The Pentecost movements that followed launched the first-century church across Palestine, the Roman Empire, Africa, India, and beyond. This Pentecost movement blended cultures, creating Creole-like communities that included Palestinian Jews, Diaspora Jews, colonial Romans, Greeks, Arabs, Samaritans, Ethiopians, and on and on. Therefore, the day of Pentecost launched the church as a multicultural and multilingual community of minority, oppressed, colonized persons who soon embraced even people from dominant and privileged groups. The first-century church was a Creole-like community. The French Caribbean writers provide a metaphorical foundation that when married to the biblical narrative of Pentecost becomes a way of living and leading for faith communities today.

THE CREOLE METAPHOR

The French Creole celebrated by the authors of *Éloge de la Créolité* emerged in its various forms primarily in French colonies in the Caribbean islands of Guadeloupe, Martinique, Saint-Barthélemy, Saint Lucia, Dominica, and other islands, as well as the South American coastal French Guiana. This particular Antillean form of French Creole provides a metaphor for this book. Sociologist Stuart Hall speaks of the origins of Creole:

> Originally, creoles were, of course, white Europeans born in the colonies, or those Europeans who had lived so long in the colonial setting, that they acquired many "native" characteristics and were thought by their European peers to have forgotten how to be "proper" Englishmen and Frenchmen. Shortly thereafter, the term came also to be applied to black slaves. The distinction in any eighteenth-century plantation document listing the slaves employed on an estate or owned by a particular slaveholder marked the distinction between "Africans" and "creoles"; and much hung on it in terms of how well "seasoned" to local conditions the slave was, how far already acclimatized to the harsh circumstances and rituals of plantation life. "Africans" were slaves who were born in Africa and transported to the colonies; "creoles" were slaves born in, and thus "native to," the island or territory. The essential distinction is between those from cultures imported from elsewhere and those rooted or grounded in the vernacular local space.[7]

The word Creole "had both a white and black referent" in the Caribbean. Over time Creole came to be understood as the result of racial mixing. Hall further elaborates that creolization is a forced "cohabitation in the colonial context [that] refers to the processes of 'cultural and linguistic mixing,' which arise from the entanglement of different cultures in the same indigenous space or location, primarily in the context of slavery, colonization and the plantation societies characteristic of the Caribbean."[8] The creolization process in the French Caribbean has created cultures defined by "their 'mixed' character, their creative vibrancy, their complex, troubled, unfinished relation to history, the prevalence in their narratives of the themes of voyaging, exile and the unrequited trauma of violent expropriation and separation." These cultures exhibit "traces of the original, but in such a way that the original is impossible to restore."[9] In the process of cohabitation in the colonial context something new was born that transformed power dynamics and shifted cultural identities.

Folklorists Robert Baron and Ana C. Cara add that "people who met speaking mutually unintelligible tongues developed a linguistic medium to communicate among themselves. They restructured the existing languages of the colonizers and colonized, [and] deeply expressive of their corresponding new cultures, pointed not only to new cultural forms but to new power relations and aesthetic dimensions."[10] The authors of *Éloge de la Créolité* define the French Caribbean Creole culture of today this way: "We are at once Europe, Africa, and enriched by Asian contributions, we are also Levantine, Indians, as well as pre-Columbian Americans in some respects. . . . So that, concerning Creoleness . . . we say that it ought to be approached as *a question to be lived*. . . . For our complexity is the very principle of our identity."[11] The formation of Creole culture is creative, combustible, and without static boundaries. Baron and Cara state, "Creole forms are expressions of culture in transition and transformation, [which] embody multiplicity, render multivocality, and negotiate contestation while also serving as means of national identity and creative expression. . . . We must recognize that there is no one creolity or single way of being Creole."[12] Patrick Chamoiseau, Raphaël Confiant, and Jean Bernabé, joined by anthropologist Lucien Taylor in "Créolité Bites," add, "Creolization is chaos—shock, mixture, combination, alchemy. . . . In creolization, there never comes a time of general synthesis, with everyone beatifically at one with one another."[13]

The authors of *Éloge de la Créolité* offer a future global definition of Creole cultural identity:

> A new humanity will gradually emerge which will have the same characteristics as our Creole humanity: all the complexity of Creoleness. The son or daughter of a German and a Haitian, born and living in Peking, will be torn between several languages, several histories, caught in the torrential ambiguity of a mosaic identity. To present creative depth, one must perceive that identity in all its complexity. He or she will be in the situation of a Creole.[14]

Their description of today's possibilities rings true to what was happening in first-century congregations as Jews cohabited in community with Romans, Greeks, and others. The first-century church developed a Creole-like expression, a shared hybrid culture. First, the Jews themselves were descended from the Hebrew people, who were of a mixed Afro-Asiatic ancestry—Africans, Asians, and indigenous Canaanites.[15] Then, with the addition of Samaritans, Greeks, Romans, Ethiopians, and others in these faith communities, a blended culture emerged. The status inversion that occurred as oppressed Jews served in leadership over Greeks and Romans meant that these faith communities addressed and reversed power dynamics.[16] Therefore, they were more than cultural hybrid communities; they were fully creolized. Faith communities in the twenty-first century must consider what it means to embrace what the authors of *Éloge de la Créolité* call "being in the situation of a Creole."

THE PROCESS OF CREOLIZATION

Creole culture and identity emerges in societies, communities, and individuals as the result of a formation process. Creolization is best understood as "culture building rather than cultural mixing or cultural blending."[17] Creolization is a formation process birthed from a certain set of circumstances, which produces a particular kind of outcomes. Creolization is a response to oppression and colonization that has great potential to restore identity and engender self-acceptance, heal and humanize individuals and communities, and revolutionize societies.

Creolization Is a Response to Oppression and Colonization

The Creole vision and reality in the French West Indies emerged out of colonization, oppression, and slavery that benefited colonial France. Colonization destroyed cultures and identities while promoting racialized and economic hierarchies. Law professor Jeannie Suk notes that "the displacement from Africa and the relocation into slavery [was] fundamentally a problem of unrepresentability that results in a situation of historylessness."[18] Bernabé, Chamoiseau, and Confiant state, "It is a terrible condition to perceive one's interior architecture, one's world, the instants of one's days, one's own values, with the eyes of the other."[19] A generation prior to the authors of *Éloge de la Créolité*, French Caribbean writers Aimé Césaire and his student Frantz Fanon commented on the effects of colonialism. Césaire spoke of how colonialism created societies "drained of their essence, cultures trampled underfoot, institutions undermined, lands confiscated, religions smashed, magnificent artistic creations destroyed, extraordinary possibilities wiped out."[20] Fanon stated that "colonized people [were] people in whose soul an inferiority complex has been created by the death and burial of its local cultural originality."[21] Bernabé, Chamoiseau, and Confiant lament that their sense of identity was invalidated by "having only the Other's pupils under one's eyelids. . . . French ways forced us to denigrate ourselves: the common condition of colonized people, [which resulted in] the quasi-complete acquisition of another identity."[22] Caribbean history was "shipwrecked in colonial history. . . . Caribbean history is just the history of the colonization of the Caribbeans."[23]

As colonization crushed cultures and maligned people's sense of identity, simultaneously oppressed human beings began to form a creolization process. Sociologists Robin Cohen and Paola Toninato note that "from a social scientist's perspective the process of cultural creolization testifies to human resilience and creativity under extreme conditions, such as those encountered in colonial societies."[24] Political scientist François Vergès speaks to the creative agency of oppressed people: "Slaves answered the hegemony of the slave system with creolization. Creolization was a process of cultural mixing in a context of slavery and colonization, a necessary adaptation to the unknown and uncharted territories of bondage, a third space of cultural expression."[25] Stuart Hall writes, "In creolization, the process of 'fusion' occurs in circumstances of massive disparities of power and the exercise of a brutal cultural dominance and incorporation between the different cultural elements. . . . Creolization is always inscribed within power relations."[26]

Philosopher Édouard Glissant adds a word of hope: "Within this universe of domination and oppression, of silent or professed dehumanization, forms of humanity stubbornly persisted."[27] The authors of *Éloge de la Créolité* also speak of resiliency and newness born of struggle. They write,

> Creoleness is the *interactional or transactional aggregate* of Caribbean, European, African, Asian, and Levantine cultural elements, united on the same soil by the yoke of history. For three centuries the islands and parts of continents affected by this phenomenon proved to be the real forges of a new humanity, where languages, races, religions, customs, ways of being from all over the world were brutally uprooted and transplanted in an environment where they had to reinvent life.[28]

As I have already stated, Christianity was born in the crucible of the colonization of Jews and others by the Roman Empire. Roman colonization was brutal. The empire occupied Palestine and ruled other provinces with the state-sponsored terror of crucifixion. Thousands of Jews were executed in this manner to strike fear in the hearts of subjects of the empire with the goal of preventing resistance and rebellion. Yet the resiliency of Jesus of Nazareth and his early followers breathed life into communities under duress and oppression. They created, as Glissant above states, "forms of humanity [that] stubbornly persisted."

Creolization Restores Identity and Engenders Self-Acceptance

Patrick Chamoiseau, Raphaël Confiant, Jean Bernabé, and Lucien Taylor in "Créolité Bites" sum up the psychic effect of colonial oppression: "While we declared ourselves to be Negroes, we were slowly becoming white, Western, dysfunctional, and anaesthetized."[29] Colonization and oppression are "a continuing psychic experience that has to be dealt with long after the actual colonial situation formally 'ends.'"[30] Therefore, there was a need to restore that which had been stripped, mutilated, and destroyed. In the 1930s a movement called Négritude emerged among post-colonialists in the French-speaking world. Martinique's Aimé Césaire was the strongest voice in the Caribbean. The authors of *Éloge de la Créolité* write concerning Césaire and Négritude in the French Caribbean,

> To a totally racist world, self-mutilated by its own colonial surgeries, Aimé Césaire restored mother African, matrix Africa, the black civilization. . . . Césaire's Négritude gave Creole society its African dimension. . . . Assimilation, through its pomps and works of Europe, tried unrelentingly to portray our lives with the colors of Elsewhere. . . . Césairian Négritude is a baptism, the primal act of our restored dignity.[31]

Creolization emerges out of oppression and colonization, births a persistent resolve to survive, and then reverses the effects of dehumanization. A postcolonial read of the New Testament writers discerns how they witnessed to the ways that Jewish identity, becoming increasingly restricted and damaged under Roman life, was being reconstituted. Jesus first went to the Jews (Matt 15:22–28; Mark 7:24–30), and the Pentecost preachers first went to Jewish communities as strategies to restore Jewish identity. The apostle Paul sought to maintain his Jewish identity in spite of his upbringing as a colonial subject, proclaiming that he was "circumcised on the eighth day, a member of the people of Israel, of the tribe of Benjamin, a Hebrew born of Hebrews; as to the law, a Pharisee" (Phil 3:5). These first-century attempts at reclaiming a Jewish identity that had been mutilated by Roman colonial surgeries were like the process of Négritude in the French colonial territories. In the recent history of the United States, members of the black community embraced Négritude-like strategies in the 1960s and 1970s, declaring "Black Power" and "Black Is Beautiful." More recently the refrain has been "Black Lives Matter."

In colonial and oppressive societies, the captive population often faces an intentional process of culture stripping and forced assimilation into dominant culture. Creolization reverses this process and restores that which was demeaned, denied, and destroyed. The authors of "Créolité Bites" write, "Césaire did effect an extraordinary change in conscious-ness, in that he reconstituted the black part of ourselves, without which we wouldn't be Creole. You can't be Creole in the Americas if you don't recognize that Africa and the African dimension is fundamental to who we are." But as we know from the definitions, Creole is not a singular cultural or racial identity. The authors of "Créolité Bites" continue, "But you've got to realize that [blackness is] only one of the forces at play in the dynamo of our identity. . . . Diasporic discourse shouldn't override indigenous discourse. It should be a complementary vision."[32] In other words, there are three primary identity dimensions of Creole culture in the Caribbean: the indigenous, the restored blackness from the African diaspora, and the remaining elements of the decolonized European. All three must be claimed and integrated into identity.

Oppressed people who have been assimilated into the culture of those dominating them must gain liberation from the identity that has been imposed on them. This is the first step in grasping onto a decolonized identity. Édouard Glissant states,

> The conquered or visited peoples are thus forced into a long and painful quest after an identity whose first task will be opposition to the denaturing process introduced by the conqueror. . . . Whole populations have had to assert their identity in opposition to the processes of identification or anni-hilation triggered by these invaders. . . . For colonized people identity will be primarily "opposed to"—that is, a limitation from the beginning.

He is saying that an oppositional identity—that is, one formed in what one is not—can limit one's ability to find one's authentic identity. Glis-sant adds, "Decolonization will have done its real work when it goes beyond this limit."[33] Decolonization began for Caribbean subjects with being set free from an imposed French identity and reclaiming a black African sense of self. Reclaiming blackness was a significant and essential move beyond the limitation of only being "not French." However, it did not address the other elements that contributed to one's culture, his-tory, and identity. Decolonization is not complete until it embraces and transforms all human elements in the local reality. While one could not reclaim identity without first embracing Africa and blackness, it was not the end of the journey.

The result of the process of creolization, according to Robin Cohen and Paola Toninato, is that it

> undermines primordial ideas of purity, race and ethnicity because it points to the existence and growing numbers of people of mixed heritage or affiliations. It challenges territorial and language-based notions of nationalism. It questions, finally, narrow religious fundamentalisms, as creolization illustrates the syncretic nature of most belief systems rather than their supposedly divine origins.[34]

A similar creolization process occurred as first-century Christian communities moved beyond a singular focus on Jewish identity re-formation and welcomed Romans and Greeks into their newly formed faith communities. A Creole-like identity formation was embraced in these new congregations. One can observe in the New Testament the ways a new communal identity was in formation as they negotiated circumcision rites, meat offered to idols, table fellowship, and the like (Acts 15:1–20).

The authors of *Éloge de la Créolité* remind us that the restoration of an authentic understanding of identity includes a deep and powerful self-acceptance, which "defeats, first of all, the old French imagery we are covered with, and restores us to ourselves in a mosaic renewed by the autonomy of its components, their unpredictability, their now mysterious resonances [and] the unconditional acceptance of our Creoleness."[35] The apostle Paul described his own self-acceptance of decolonized and reclaimed identities when he wrote, "We regard no one from a human point of view" (2 Cor 5:16). He was saying that he no longer regarded himself or anyone else from a dominant, Roman-Empire point of view, that is as colonizer or colonized.[36]

Creolization Heals and Humanizes

The restoration of identity and resulting self-acceptance offers a healing that rehumanizes individuals and communities. Literary critic Wilson Harris calls this the "saving nemesis" of creolization. He writes, "*Creoleness* signifies mixed race and a cross-cultural nemesis capable of becoming a saving nemesis. *Saving nemesis* may also be a peculiar expression, but it implies recuperative powers and vision within a scale of violence that is dismembering societies around the globe."[37] Harris's phrase "saving nemesis" suggests that what colonization meant for destruction was transformed by creolization into something life giving. Literature professors Kathleen M. Balutansky and Marie-Agnés Sourieau confirm this notion: "It is from this dynamic that creolization becomes a power for reversing the processes of acculturation (or assimilation), deculturation, discontinuity, and marginalization that have affected the entire Caribbean."[38]

In the New Testament, the story of Jesus's death and resurrection acts as a "saving nemesis." The crucifixion of Jesus was meant to be an act of brutal finality by the Roman Empire. Yet this nemesis act was reversed by a more powerful and completely just God into an act of salvation. Biblical scholars John Crossan and Jonathan Reed write, "It was not simply death and resurrection. It was execution by *Rome* and therefore resurrection against *Rome*."[39] Those first-century Pentecost preachers' declaration of the cross and resurrection of Jesus was an audacious claim that in the face of the terror of colonization God brought forth new life—a saving nemesis. Allan Boesak and I write in *Radical Reconciliation* that the logic of the church's

> proclamation is that because death by Rome was reversed through resurrection by God, the death of one's identity could be revived and returned to full humanity. All identities—ethnic, gender, religious, and the like—were reframed in one's self-definition. One's colonial identity was switched to an identity in Jesus Christ. The language used for Caesar—"Son of God," "Lord," "Redeemer," "Savior," "Liberator," "God"—Paul used for Jesus Christ, to announce a new identity.[40]

The death of Jesus was a saving and resurrecting nemesis. Crossan and Reed write, "In a world where identity was often shaped by one's relationship to Rome, by being, as it were, 'in Rome,' insisting on a self-definition exclusively by being 'in Christ' was subversive at best and treasonous at worst."[41]

In *Pedagogy of the Oppressed*, educator Paulo Freire called dehumanization "a *distortion* of the vocation of becoming more fully human [and] the result of an unjust order that engenders violence in the oppressors, which in turn dehumanizes the oppressed."[42] Dehumanization is complete when a person is dependent on the oppressor for her or his identity. Freire observed that often for oppressed persons "their ideal is to be [human]; but for them, to be [human] is to be oppressors. This is their model for humanity."[43] So colonized and oppressed people must be rehumanized. Creolization is "the unceasing process of transformation of political, religious, social, and cultural elements constantly acting upon one another or humanizing one another."[44] The same is true for former oppressors and privileged people. When privileged people "cease to be exploiters or indifferent spectators or simply the heirs of exploitation and move to the side of the exploited, they almost always bring with them the marks of their origin."[45] Oppressors and privileged people have also been dehumanized and will need to be creolized to be rehumanized (we will revisit this point in chap. 5). Creolization releases a saving nemesis that heals and humanizes both the oppressed and those benefiting from oppression.

Creolization Revolutionizes Society

Robert Baron and Ana C. Cara declare, "Creole enactments are counterhegemonic in their challenge to cultural dominance, making creolity nothing but revolutionary."[46] A process that responds to oppression with the purpose of restoring identity and humanizing oppressed people must be a revolutionary process. Folklorist Roger D. Abrahams adds, "Indeed, in class-ridden situations, creolized expressive forms take on a derisive charge leveled at elites and function as a form of resistance from below."[47] Baron and Cara state that creolization voices "alternative ways of being to those imposed hegemonically by colonial powers and elite cultural forces. Formulated and enacted by folks who historically lacked political power yet aimed to establish autonomy, Creole cultural forms have often been subversive social and political tools."[48]

The apostle Paul writes in Ephesians 2 that Jesus created "in himself one new humanity in place of the two, thus making peace, and might reconcile both groups to God in one body through the cross" (2:15b–16a). Not only was the cross transformed from a Roman form of terror into a saving nemesis, it revolutionized society. The passage states that in place of two categories of humanity—the powerful (Romans and Greeks) and the oppressed (Jews along with other colonized people)—a qualitatively different understanding of humanity was implemented. Ephesians 2 declared a revolution of human identity from colonial to Creole. It signaled to society that patriarchy, class status, racial hierarchies, and other systemic forms of classifying humanity for domination were replaced by a new structure of "one new humanity." Paulo Freire wrote, "The man or woman who emerges is a new person, viable only as the oppressor-oppressed contradiction is superseded by the humanization of all people."[49]

Creolization is a revolutionary act in society. As the authors of *Éloge de la Créolité* write, "At the heart of our Creoleness we will maintain the modulation of new rules, of illicit blendings. For we know that each culture is never a finished product but rather the constant dynamics on the lookout for genuine issues, new possibilities, and interested in relating rather than dominating, in exchanging rather than looting."[50]

CREOLE-LIKE CONGREGATIONS IN THE TWENTY-FIRST CENTURY

In chapter 2, the theory and theology of creolization moves into the practical and present reality. Middle Collegiate Church in the East Village of New York City is part of the four-congregation collective of Collegiate Churches on the isle of Manhattan that are the oldest continuous Christian congregations in the United States. Started by Dutch colonizers in the Reformed tradition, Middle Collegiate Church is now one of the most diverse congregations in the United States. The story of this Creole-like congregation is told by its current senior minister, Dr. Jacqueline J. Lewis, an African American woman who has curated this amazing process of creolization.

Notes

1. Richard A. Horsley, *Jesus and Empire: The Kingdom of God and the New World Order* (Minneapolis: Fortress, 2003), 21.

2. For an expanded discussion of first-century decolonized reconciliation, see Allan Aubrey Boesak and Curtiss Paul DeYoung, *Radical Reconciliation: Beyond Political Pietism and Christian Quietism* (Maryknoll, NY: Orbis, 2012), 12–23.

3. The biblical word for reconciliation in Greek is *katallassō*. It literally means "to exchange places." See Boesak and DeYoung, *Radical Reconciliation*, 12.

4. Boesak and DeYoung, *Radical Reconciliation*, 80–82.

5. Jean Bernabé, Patrick Chamoiseau, and Raphaël Confiant, *Éloge de la Créolité / In Praise of Creoleness*, Édition Bilingue (Paris: Gallimard, 1993), 75.

6. Roy Chandler Caldwell Jr., "Créolité and Postcoloniality in Raphaël Confiant's L'Allées des Soupirs," in *The French Review* 73, no. 2 (Dec. 1999): 302.

7. Stuart Hall, "Créolité and the Process of Creolization," in Robin Cohen and Paola Toninato, eds., *The Creolization Reader: Studies in Mixed Identities and Cultures* (London: Routledge, 2010), 27–28.

8. Hall, "Créolité and the Process of Creolization," 28.

9. Hall, "Créolité and the Process of Creolization," 28, 29.

10. Robert Baron and Ana C. Cara, "Introduction: Creolization as Cultural Creativity," in *Creolization as Cultural Creativity*, ed. Robert Baron and Ana C. Cara (Jackson: University Press of Mississippi, 2011), 3.

11. Bernabé et al., *Éloge de la Créolité*, 88–90.

12. Baron and Cara, "Introduction: Creolization as Cultural Creativity," 3, 5.

13. Patrick Chamoiseau, Raphaël Confiant, Jean Bernabé, and Lucien Taylor, "Créolité Bites: A Conversation with Patrick Chamoiseau, Raphaël Confiant, and Jean Bernabé," *Transition* 74 (1997): 136.

14. Bernabé et al., *Éloge de la Créolité*, 112.

15. For Jews/Hebrews as "Afro-Asiatics" see Curtiss Paul DeYoung, *Coming Together in the 21st Century: The Bible's Message in an Age of Diversity* (Valley Forge, PA: Judson, 2009), 14–16, 53–54. Also see Cain Hope Felder, *Troubling Biblical Waters: Race, Class, and Family* (Maryknoll, NY: Orbis, 1989), 37.

16. See "status inversion" in Boesak and DeYoung, *Radical Reconciliation*, 82–83.

17. Sidney Mintz, "The Localization of Anthropological Practice: From Area Studies to Transnationalism," *Critique of Anthropology* 18, no. 119 (1998), quoted in Baron and Cara, "Introduction: Creolization as Cultural Creativity," 7.

18. Jeannie Suk, *Postcolonial Paradoxes in French Caribbean Writing: Césaire, Glissant, Condé* (New York: Oxford, 2003), 74.

19. Bernabé et al., *Éloge de la Créolité*, 76.

20. Aimé Césaire, *Discourse on Colonialism*, rev. ed. (New York: Monthly Review Press, 2000), 43.

21. Frantz Fanon, *Black Skin, White Masks* (New York: Grove, 1967), 18.

22. Bernabé et al., *Éloge de la Créolité*, 85–87.

23. Bernabé et al., *Éloge de la Créolité*, 98.

24. Robin Cohen and Paola Toninato, "The Creolization Debate: Analyzing Mixed Identities and Cultures," in Cohen and Toninato, *Creolization Reader*, 12.

25. Françoise Vergés, "Kiltir Kreol: Processes and Practices of Créolité and Creolization," in Okwui Enwezor et al., *Créolité and Creolization* (Ostfildern-Ruit, Germany: Hatje Cantz, 2003), 180.

26. Stuart Hall, "Creolization, Diaspora, and Hybridity in the Context of Globalization," in Enwezor et al., *Créolité and Creolization*, 186.

27. Édouard Glissant, *Poetics of Relation* (Ann Arbor: The University of Michigan Press, 1997), 65.

28. Bernabé et al., *Éloge de la Créolité*, 87–88.

29. Chamoiseau et al., "Créolité Bites," 158.

30. Kathleen M. Balutansky and Marie-Agnès Sourieau, introduction to *Caribbean Creolization: Reflections on the Cultural Dynamics of Language, Literature, and Identity*, ed. Kathleen M. Balutansky and Marie-Agnès Sourieau (Gainesville: University Press of Florida, 1998), 5–6.

31. Bernabé et al., *Éloge de la Créolité*, 79–80.

32. Chamoiseau et al., "Créolité Bites," 145, 151.

33. Glissant, *Poetics of Relation*, 17.

34. Cohen and Toninato, "Creolization Debate," 16.

35. Bernabé et al., *Éloge de la Créolité*, 86, 87.

36. Boesak and DeYoung, *Radical Reconciliation*, 17.

37. Wilson Harris, "Creoleness: The Crossroads of a Civilization?," in Balutansky and Sourieau, *Caribbean Creolization*, 26.

38. Balutansky and Sourieau, introduction to *Caribbean Creolization*, 5.

39. John Dominic Crossan and Jonathan L. Reed, *In Search of Paul: How Jesus's Apostle Opposed Rome's Empire with God's Kingdom* (San Francisco: HarperSanFrancisco, 2004), 384.

40. Boesak and DeYoung, *Radical Reconciliation*, 17.

41. Crossan and Reed, *In Search of Paul*, 280.

42. Paulo Freire, *Pedagogy of the Oppressed* (New York: Continuum, 2000), 44.

43. Freire, *Pedagogy of the Oppressed*, 45.

44. Kathleen M. Balutansky and Marie-Agnés Sourieau, "Part One: Creolization and the Creative Imagination," in Balutansky and Sourieau, *Caribbean Creolization*, 21.

45. Freire, *Pedagogy of the Oppressed*, 60.

46. Baron and Cara, "Introduction: Creolization as Cultural Creativity," 6.

47. Roger D. Abrahams, "About Face: Rethinking Creolization," in Baron and Cara, *Creolization as Cultural Creativity*, 286.

48. Baron and Cara, "Introduction: Creolization as Cultural Creativity," 6.

49. Freire, *Pedagogy of the Oppressed*, 49.

50. Bernabé et al., *Éloge de la Créolité*, 114.

2.

Middle Collegiate Church: Creolization in the East Village

JACQUELINE J. LEWIS

Why is eleven o'clock on Sunday morning still, too often, the most seg-regated hour in America? This is the question that drove me back to graduate school at Drew University. I wanted to study racial identity development; I wanted to know what kind of leadership was required to build multiethnic, multicultural communities of faith that could dis-rupt white supremacy and racism in our nation. While working on my PhD dissertation about leadership in multiracial congregations, I discov-ered Middle Collegiate Church in the East Village of New York City. I went to visit on Easter Sunday in 2002. Before I walked in the door, I knew something was different. There was a jazz band playing music on the narrow front lawn. On the steps was a black woman with gray, curly hair and a young white man, both warm and friendly. I received a handshake from the man and a warm embrace from the woman, Danita, who would become one of my dear friends.

Once inside the heavy wooden doors, I was in awe of the beautiful old, traditional sanctuary, with dark wood ceilings, oak pews covered in red cushions, and a large marble pulpit bedecked with a green pillow, placed there in case the preacher needs a place to lean between para-graphs. Gold-leaf stenciling adorned the warm, peach walls; the only cross in the building was lusciously stenciled behind the pulpit. Tiffany stained glass windows depicted stories of Jesus with children and women. As worship began, a biracial gospel choir rocked, "I need you to survive." A classical choir sang Handel's "Halleluiah Chorus," and a friendly, white, middle-aged pastor named Gordon Dragt managed to preach a sermon about hope after death without mentioning the resurrection. I loved the worship.

When it was over, Gordon found me in the fellowship hall, all smiles and warmth. He found me simply because I was new. I told him about my study and asked if I could come and interview him and his people. He enthusiastically agreed. I spent months visiting Middle Church, listening to people's stories, hearing their hopes and dreams. I fell in love with these people who shared a passion for life in a congregation in which everyone is welcome just as they are as they come through the door.[1]

The following year on Martin Luther King Jr. Day, I was invited to preach to these lovely people. I celebrated Middle Church. "If there is a heaven, and I believe there is, it must look like this. You look like heaven to me! You don't have to be here. You could be in the so-called white church; you could be in the so-called black church. But here you are. Black, white, some Latinos—choosing to be together in this place." One woman, Gloria Moy, shouted, "What about Asian; what about Chinese?" I said from the pulpit, "My bad, you are right. Black, white, Asian, Latino, Native American—all here together, looking like heaven to me."

By June 2003, I had received a call from Middle Collegiate Church to serve as the Collegiate Associate Minister for eighteen months with Gordon Dragt and to remain as Senior Minister in Charge upon his retirement—the first woman and the first person of color in the senior position in the long history of the Collegiate Church, which was formed in 1628. Here was my dream come true: a church living out my hopes for a multiethnic, multicultural future. True, Middle Church was predominately white with a growing black community in those days. But it looked like a promise. It looked like a community fully welcoming of folks from many social locations. It looked like a place fully inclusive of LGBTQI people and their families. It looked like a place that celebrated the arts. It looked like a place boldly embodying personal faith and public proclamation of justice as its way of being. I was hooked, because to me Middle Church looked like heaven on earth.

Before hiring me in January 2004, the consistory (our board) had done important work on identity and vision. They had asked the question, "What is the essential Middle Church?" They believed that core to Middle Church's identity was the radically welcoming personality of Gordon Dragt, who had been at Middle Church for twenty-five years. They also knew that it had something to do with history, values, and location. During the 1980s, when thousands of people were dying of AIDS in the East Village of Manhattan, Middle Church was the safe place to gather for funerals. On September 11, 2001, Middle Church was the safe place for people making their way north from Ground Zero, covered in ash and tears. Radical welcome and justice works were in their DNA. Through one-to-one conversations and in focus groups guided by prayer, leaders listened for the hopes, dreams, and the call of the congregation. When they pondered what Middle Church would look like in fifteen years, the consistory adopted this vision statement in March 2005:

> Middle Collegiate Church is a celebrating, culturally diverse, inclusive and growing community of faith where all persons are welcomed just as they are as they come through the door. Rooted in Christian tradition as the oldest continuous Protestant Church in North America, Middle Church is called by God to boldly do a new thing on the earth. As a teaching congregation that celebrates the arts, our ministries include rich and meaningful worship, care and education that nurture the mind, body, and spirit, social action which embraces the global community, and participation in interfaith dialogue for the purpose of justice and reconciliation.

In 2018, having already accomplished what we had hoped to see in 2020, the staff and consistory of Middle Church adopted this Vision Statement to take us to 2025:

> Middle Collegiate Church is a multicultural, multiethnic, intergenerational movement of Spirit and justice, powered by Revolutionary Love, with room for all. Following in the Way of Jesus' radical love, and inspired by the prophets, Middle Church is called by God to do a bold new thing on the earth. We aim to heal the soul and the world by dismantling racist, classist, sexist, and homophobic systems of oppression. Because our God is still speaking in many languages, we work in inter-religious partnerships to uproot injustice, eradicate poverty, care for the brokenhearted, and build the Reign of God on earth. This activism is fueled by our faith; our faith is expressed in art; our art is an active prayer connecting us with the Holy Spirit. Middle Church affirms the transformative power of moral imagination, reclaiming and reframing Christianity inside our walls, on the street, and in virtual spaces around the globe.

Even though our vision statement has changed, we remain clear that we are called to do a bold new thing on the earth and that all people—no matter their race/ethnicity, gender/gender performance, sexual orientation, age, or position in life—are precious to God, welcome in our community, and awesomely and wonderfully made in the image of God (Genesis 1, 2; Psalm 139). We believe God is indeed doing a new thing in and through us (Isa 43:19). This statement says something about not only our vision but our ongoing sense of identity.

CREOLIZATION IN THE EAST VILLAGE

Core to the identity of Middle Church is a sense of radical welcome, the welcome Jesus offered to strangers, so-called sinners, women, children, and those on the margins. No matter whom you love, no matter how you look, no matter how you make your living—you are welcome. Not only that, our clergy, board members, and lay leaders are intentionally recruited to reflect our commitment to racial/ethnic, gender/sexuality, and cultural diversity. Our worship and our programming use the arts to communicate the radical love and welcome of God in a way that drops us right into deep experiences of hope and revolutionary love. And we believe that our relationship to the Holy One means boldly working to create a more just society, one in which everyone has enough. This is our calling; this is our identity. I'd like to explore now why, and how over time, we have come more fully to inhabit our welcoming, artistic, inclusive, and bold identity as a multiracial, multicultural, Creole-like church.

Let me make the connection to the creolization process as described in chapter 1, "a response to oppression and colonization that restores identity and engenders self-acceptance, heals and humanizes individuals and communities, and revolutionizes societies." This is what happens at Middle Church. When I say welcoming, I mean that our culture, our ethos, is a warm, welcome embrace full of joy. Visitors are treated like members, not strangers. We are certainly a congregation of people who have experienced oppression. Our congregational culture is born out of the reality of injustice experienced by people of color, women, and our LGBTQI community. Many people in our congregation have been wounded by life in other congregations. We restore identity and self-acceptance through our radical love and inclusion. We are intentional about how we hire, who leads, the language we use, the way we treat children, and how many voices are at the table. We are LGBTQI-welcoming and womanist in orientation. We experience healing and promote humanizing through worship and the arts, and more and more in small groups and in classes. And we are bold and revolutionary through protest, community organizing, interreligious alliances, and the like.

A WELCOME SHAPED BY OVERCOMING OPPRESSION

When I came to Middle Church in 2004, we were mostly white, with a nice-sized community of African American members. There were about ten Latinx and two or three Chinese members. One of them was a spunky, smart woman named Gloria, whom I mentioned earlier. Anytime we named our diversity, "We are black, white, Latino . . . ," she exclaimed, "Don't forget *Asian*." Her critique led to a one-on-one conversation and a plan to celebrate Lunar New Year. I worked with Gloria, my staff, and our music team to create a Lunar New Year celebration that would work in our context. We thought it should be nontraditional and pan-Asian to celebrate the Japanese, Chinese, Korean, and Indian members of our East Village community. Gloria and Jocelyn, a lovely author who has a Chinese father and a white mother, wrote prayers. Chad, who was born in Hawaii to Japanese and Korean parents, preached. We invited a koto player to join us. Kashimi danced the Fan Dance. Gloria passed out red envelopes so we could take up a special offering for survivors of an earthquake in Japan.

Listening deeply to Gloria, I came to understand her personal story of oppression. She often feels unseen in conversations about inclusion or in work on racial reconciliation. These projects are often cast in the very real and barely-healing scars that chattel slavery left on our nation. But Chinese Americans have their own stories. Stories of prejudice and bias, economic oppression, and stereotyping. Stories of violence in the container of white supremacy that is the sad truth of our history. My work with Gloria sent me to my history books. And what we created together helped her to be seen and heard. With that, all of the folks in the congregation who are Asian in culture and heritage could claim an authentic space in Middle Church's radical welcome, along with a unique and important role in our work on racial justice.

The entire congregation was so excited to celebrate Asian cultures in this new way. Four Japanese women, led by Kaede, and one African American soprano, Tina, formed the group Rising Sun! Now, they sing every Lunar New Year celebration, which always occurs in February, when we are also celebrating African American History Month. As we have continued this tradition, our gospel choir has welcomed Asian members—Japanese, Chinese, and Vietnamese. The gospel choir looks more and more like the United Nations! The Salim family—Chinese from Indonesia—has grown, marrying and having children who are baptized. The Wu family—Mom, Dad, and three children who found us by way of an organist friend—have grown up at Middle Church. The Wu children sing in the choir and make sandwiches for our feeding ministry, and James, their dad, is an elder on our board. Watching the oldest child—Jordan—grow up and head off to college has been such a joy.

In 2017, we not only celebrated Lunar New Year, we also celebrated Pan-Asian American History month. On one May Sunday, one hundred judges and court officers from Judicial Friends—a traditionally African American and Latinx group of judges—joined us for worship. What a remarkable day. One hundred esteemed guests in black robes processed behind our two choirs. Kashimi danced a beautiful piece she had choreographed when a tsunami hit Japan. And the growing-up Wu children offered a prayer with their dad. The multicultural, multiracial identity of Middle Church was in full regalia, as colorful as Kashimi's scarf.

Because we are who we are, our Latinx family yearned for more celebration of the unique cultures they represent. So, we began using two Sundays in September and October to celebrate the many cultures of our Latinx/Hispanic family; now we honor those cultures every Sunday for five weeks! Worship, my sermon in Spanglish, education programs, and food from several Latinx cultures after worship teach Middle Church *que somos Latinos, también.* Our commitment to our Latinx family means that we are deeply committed to the rebuilding of Puerto Rico after Hurricane Maria devastated the island nation and the Virgin Islands. We have raised over $25,000 to date, and volunteers have travelled to Puerto Rico to build solar energy systems and clean-water kits, and take supplies to children and seniors. We are building a close relationship with a town called Miraflores and look forward to seeing our connection blossom.

Not only that, Middle Church has stepped boldly into the issue of immigration. As I write, there are 12,800 children still separated from their families. We have travelled to El Paso and Ciudad Juárez in partnership with Hope on the Border. We went to learn and to bear witness, so we could build a strategy to help reunite families and to insist on immigration reform. On Independence Day in 2018, we staged a protest outside one of the so-called detention centers in Manhattan. We are working with the Sanctuary Movement and adopting a family to support. We are using the social capital we have to keep these stories and these lives in the media and at the front of Americans' minds as we think of faith and electoral politics.

Rebuilding Puerto Rico and working on the border remind us that part of our family is suffering, and that means we are suffering. In partnership with our sister congregation, Fort Washington Collegiate Church, whose senior minister, Damaris Whittaker, is a Puerto Rican, we are boldly declaring that racism has many tentacles, and they reach deeply into the hearts of our Latinx family. Taking action not only helps alleviate the suffering of those *en la frontera,* wherever it may be; when we go to the border, we develop new identities. Part of our emerging identity is the sure knowledge that we are inextricably connected to one another. This connection is the spirit in a Zulu folk saying, *"Ubuntu ngumuntu nagabantu,"* meaning, "A person is a person because of other people."

What does this mean? As he approached retirement, Bishop Desmond Tutu was asked by President Nelson Mandela to chair South Africa's Truth and Reconciliation Commission, which sought to come to terms with the human rights offenses of the past in order to move into the future. In his memoir of that time period, *No Future without Forgiveness,* Tutu writes,

> Ubuntu is very difficult to render into a Western language. It speaks of the very *essence* of being human. When we want to give high praise to someone we say, "*Yu, u nobunto*"; "Hey, so-and-so has *ubuntu.*" Then you are generous, you are hospitable, you are friendly and caring and compassionate. You share what you have. It is to say, "My humanity is inextricably bound up in yours." We belong in a bundle of life.[2]

What is also helping our Creole-like congregation overcome oppression is seeing each other more clearly. According to Peter de Jager, the Zulu greeting *Sawubona* means "I see you," and the response, *Ngikhona,* means "I am here." As always when translating from one language to another, crucial subtleties are lost. Inherent in the Zulu greeting and our grateful response is the sense that until you saw me, I didn't exist. By recognizing me, you brought me into existence. Making time to create worship and rituals that acknowledge and celebrate the richness of our cultural diversity means we see each other—gifts, sorrows, hopes, joys, disappointments. Seeing is a salve, a balm in Gilead to make the wounded whole.

Middle Church celebrates Black History Month in February, but all year long we are committed to disrupting racism. We are part of the Black Lives Matter movement, and we offer a conference every year to help congregational leaders develop the capacity to grow multiracial, multiethnic congregations. We have been teaching classes for a decade on dismantling racism, but this year, we formed a Healing Racism Task Force. Whites, blacks, Latinx, and Asians were invited into a one-year learning community of reading, writing, experiencing art, and breaking bread together. Along with our cultural celebrations, this task force is intended to help create strategies to enable Middle Church to deepen our strong commitment to anti-racist work.

Our commitment to our LGBTQI family is decades long. We have a float in the Pride March every June, and in 2016 we (a *church!*) won Best Float. Our fifty-member multi-everything gospel choir rocks music down Fifth Avenue in Manhattan, while a hundred more of us dance in the streets. It is always my great joy to watch the faces of the people on the street. They see our choir singing gospel music, and they see me and my clergy colleagues wearing our "Love. Period." shirts and our clergy collars. They are surprised by our bold proclamation of a God whose name is Love, a God who created them just as they are, who loves them just as they are.

One June, as I was dancing down the street to our gospel choir's amazing music, I came alongside one of our young adults, Matt. He is a beautiful gay man with gorgeous brown skin, soulful eyes, and a smile to stop traffic. Matt and I began to dance together, laughing and singing, a joy-filled collaboration and celebration of our selves. Matt later said,

> At first, I didn't understand how a church could go to the Pride March. In my experience, churches were against gays. But on this day, I was looking at all the people on the street. I was listening to the gospel music. I was dancing with my pastor. And I thought to myself, "I am exactly who I'm supposed to be. I am exactly where I'm supposed to be. My pastor loves me, my God loves me. All is well with my soul!"

Matt's comment moves me deeply and reminds me of the multiplicity of identities that we all inhabit. Black, gay, struggling artist, son of conservative family—all of these identities come with Matt, who, having been oppressed, needed to be healed. In our congregation, he is seen, known, loved, and welcomed. This is part of his healing.

As we explored identities and cultures, we had a significant blind spot. Then at an American Academy of Religion meeting in 2010, I met a young theologian named Ivan Petrella. He was brilliant and about to take a sabbatical. I invited him to come to New York and spend time at Middle Church. Ivan offered a gentle and important critique: "Middle Church is all about justice, but you don't talk about money, and you don't talk about class. What does that mean?" How grateful I was to hear that critique and to be taught by Ivan, both by his presence in our midst and by reading his work. Middle Collegiate Church is part of the Collegiate Church of New York, five ministries that together are the oldest continuous Protestant church in North America. We were formed in 1628, before the colonies formed a nation. We have a sizeable endowment. Our silence about money is partly due to this fact and our discomfort about sharing the details. But Ivan's critique, his ability to see that about us and share it, has opened us up to see that one of the cultures at work in our congregation is class.

Middle Church sits in the East Village of Manhattan. We are bordered by SoHo, China Town, and Little Italy to the south; the Village (West) and New York University, The New School, and Cooper Union to the West; Alphabet City and housing projects to the East; and Chelsea and the Flat Iron District to the north. Our church draws people from all these spaces and from Riverdale, Harlem, the South Bronx, Brooklyn, and Queens—from all over the city and from New Jersey and Connecticut. We are lawyers, teachers, entrepreneurs, and professors; we are actors, artists, and activists. Some of us own several houses; some of us live in shelters. Some of us are philanthropists; some of us are one paycheck away from being homeless.

One way we used to deal with all this diversity was not to discuss it. We shied away from our internal diversity, even as we offered food and clothing to our even-poorer neighbors. As we have become more aware of our silence and self-consciousness, we have been forced to work to be different, to transform our silence into activism. We address individual needs with the occasional loan, referrals, and feeding programs. We address the systemic issues by fighting for a living wage, paid leave, and health care. We are partners in the Poor People's Campaign, and we campaign for voting rights and prison reform, issues we connect to the oppressive weight of poverty. We understand that feeding and clothing God's people is not enough. Through our ministry, we insist on economic justice for the people of God and use our pulpit and social media to educate our economically diverse community that everyone should have enough. We understand that economic justice begins with giving children a strong educational footing beginning with preschool. We are creating programs to support families with children so all our little people can have a healthy head start on life, and to support college students by providing books.

BUILDING A CREOLE-LIKE IDENTITY THROUGH RADICAL INCLUSION

When we boldly declare that everyone is welcome just as they are as they come through the door, when we say there is room for all at Middle Church, we mean it. Middle Church welcomes those who are differently abled, those who are poor, and those who have been disenfranchised because of how they look or how they make a living or who they love. When we say we practice radical inclusion, we mean we are rooted in the love of God, following in the way of Jesus. We feel called by God to put those who are on the margins—women, children, the poor, the formerly incarcerated, immigrants, and people struggling with mental illness; those who are aging; racial/ethnic minorities; and those who are marginalized due to their sexual orientation or gender performance—right in the center of the reign of God. This is where Jesus tells us they belong.

We announce our identity as a radically welcoming and inclusive community. This is consistently displayed on our website, in our presence in the public square, in the diversity of the staff and volunteers, and in congregational life. For many years we have, as I have mentioned, marched in the annual Pride March, supported the Black Lives Matter movement, and demonstrated against gun violence. These public actions have been key to our ability to attract a new and diverse flow of visitors, who often become constituents and then members and volunteers.

At Middle Church, we have offered adult study groups on "Erasing Racism," "Exploring Race, Class, and Culture," and "Race, Grace, and the Reign of God," all of which invite participants to explore the formative messages and lessons they received regarding race while growing up in this society. Additionally, we have convened a "Racial Healing Task Force," which has committed to a yearlong process of shared learning to engage in truth-telling, storytelling, research, and the evolution of a learning design for others who want to work at issues of race, racism, and white supremacy. We have asked participants to learn the history of the nation from its founding to the institution of slavery through Jim Crow, the civil rights movement to Ferguson, and the current movement to challenge manifestations of racism and white supremacy. We develop new leaders by helping them expand their knowledge and understanding of systemic and seemingly permanent structural racism, giving them language and voice to address difficult issues, and creating a community where this work is ongoing and normalized.

The spiritual leaders in a multicultural, multiracial setting are called to provide opportunities for the members of the faith community to deepen their understanding of each other and the impact of racism in the world around them. Understanding structural racism forces us to turn a lens on our own complacence and complicity with racist systems and the power dynamics of racial hierarchies, even in our congregations. We are awakened to the ways and times we are called to step up and then step back. Our new wisdom leads us to make space to include others.

These leaders must see themselves as students of race, culture, and the dynamics of white privilege and white supremacy. While our staff represents diverse theological perspectives—some of us more traditionally Christian and others more Universalist in our understanding of God's redemptive work in the world—we are deeply committed to using inclusive language in worship. When it makes sense, we usually use no pronouns for God, and when we must use pronouns, we alternate "he" and "she." We are also inclusive in speaking theologically about God's love shown in Jesus Christ as a wide-open door, not a litmus test that God's people can fail. Though we are Christian, we understand that God speaks many languages. We take care not to leave our non-Christian family (yes, we have members who are Jewish, humanists, and agnostics and atheists, and one Muslim member) outside of the grace we believe God is offering to us in worship and throughout congregational life. The way we think and talk about the God we worship reflects the interreligious, interfaith partnerships we participate in as we seek to repair the world. We regard the faith walks of those around us with respect and care.

Art matters for building a Creole-like community at Middle Church. We express our yearning to participate in God's plan for healing our souls and the world in our music and in the arts. Once a theme has been chosen for a season of worship, the minister who will preach each Sunday during the season selects a focus text—usually one from the Revised Common Lectionary—and shares the text, a sermon title, and a few sentences expressing what the sermon promises to do. With this summary, the music and worship team and I begin to think of creative ways to express in worship and the arts our yearning to be part of God's plan for humanity, attending to this sermon as well as the worship arc of the year.

We choose music from all eras of traditional Western church music, from cultures representative of members of our congregation, and from cultures that may evoke fresh understandings of God. For example, "This Is Me" from the movie *The Greatest Showman* has a particular resonance for Pride Month. "Glory" from the movie *Selma* has power in Black History Month but also at Christmas time. A beautiful Kenyan religious folk song, "Wana Baraka," might be sung at Pentecost, its Kenyan lyrics alternating with "halleluiah," making it both strange and familiar. We even include music from Broadway shows that fit a specific theme. All styles, in other words, are welcome. We also consider not only the liturgical calendar but also secular calendars, noting things like World AIDS Day; African American, Asian American, or Latinx History Months; Pride Month; Women's History Month; Labor Day; Native

American Day; Memorial Day; Independence Day; and Juneteenth. We use our holy imaginations and everything from tap dance to puppetry in worship so that it dramatizes and rehearses the story we believe God is writing with humankind. We also use worship to disrupt the dominant narrative in the world. For example, on the Sunday before Columbus Day, we commemorate Indigenous people and their contributions. We do this because we know that Christopher Columbus did not discover America but rather happened upon a land that was already inhabited.

Multiracial and multicultural communities will not thrive with unimaginative worship that represents only one culture. Our musicians, clergy, staff, and lay artists must all share the congregation's vision for racial/ethnic and cultural diversity and have capacities to enact it. Worship needs to address the living texts of congregants living in a complex world. Time for mourning happens in prayer; time for activism happens when we wear hoodies in solidarity with Trayvon Martin and other young boys of color or take worship to the street in the Pride March each year. Worship puts our living texts, the cultural texts, and the sacred narrative in conversation, making meaning of individual lives, culture, and world—and transforming them all.

In Creole-like faith communities, issues of race, class, sexuality, and gender cannot be avoided. It is likely that in such faith communities, unintended racial and cultural offenses that generate hurt feelings, frustration, and anger will accumulate over time if they are not discussed openly. When this happens, people will either quietly disappear or challenge congregational "harmony" by expressing how they feel but doing so in unhelpful ways. A congregation cannot be truly diverse and inclusive without talking about the most sensitive issues of race, class, sexuality, and gender. Such conversations must be ongoing and firmly woven into the life of the congregation. Structured conversations in a safe setting can be educational, healing, and freeing.

At Middle Church, great care and intentionality are practiced when facilitating these conversations. For example, I invited a diverse group of participants to commit to a yearlong process of study, conversation, and healing focused on white supremacy, racial bias, and racism. The gatherings included viewings of *RIKERS: An American Jail,* a documentary by Bill Moyers; *I Am Not Your Negro*, based on the words of James Baldwin; and Ava DuVernay's documentary *13th.* Together we read James Baldwin's *The Fire Next Time,* a letter to his nephew; and Ta-Nehisi Coates's *Between the World and Me,* a letter to his son. Members of the group were then asked to write their own letter to someone important to them, expressing their thoughts, hopes, and experiences regarding race. Additionally, four or five group members of the same ethnicity were invited into a "fishbowl," to sit together in the center of the room while other task force members encircled them. First, those identifying as African American came to the center of the room to respond to the question, "What do you say about race when people of another ethnicity are not around?" Next, a group identifying more generally as "persons of color" followed by a group of individuals identifying as white each sat in the center to discuss the same question. This experience was profound for many of us. We encountered the conversation we rarely hear from one another. Such structured conversations can be held once the group has developed a sense of trust and all have agreed to a shared set of norms for how the learning community will do its work.

COMMUNICATION ON THE BORDER

Influenced by the work of Virgilio Elizondo, W. E. B. Du Bois, and Donald Winnicott, I have come to call these kinds of conversations "communication on the border." Leaders on the border in multiracial congregations must on the one hand speak truth to power (prophetic speech) and on the other comfort God's people in an experimental border space (pastoral speech). Communication on the border requires language in newsletters, sermons, prayers, and elsewhere that contests and critiques injustice, hegemony, and discrimination. And at the same time, often in the same settings and media, leaders must use language that affirms the people in the congregation—their individual experiences, their journeys, their courage to be on the border, and their hopes, dreams, and fears. This is the both/and language of the prophets. On the one hand we ask, Can you see that God is with us, doing a bold new thing in us, using us in the service of healing? On the other hand, we lament with the suffering over how broken our world is, how painful it is, and how often we feel that God is absent or not present enough.

What does this both/and look like? Let me give you one example from Pride Sunday in 2017. The morning prayer at Middle Church is our prayer of intercession, our prayers of the people. Pride Sunday is such an upbeat day. The music is lively, often pulled from both sacred and secular sources. Before the sermon, a beautiful anthem acknowledged God's love for all of us. The hymns evoked confidence in God's love of all humanity. After my prayer, one choir was scheduled to sing a text that gave thanks for God's presence in every breath we take. Along with all the joy in the room, however, there was grief. We remembered the anniversaries of the murders at Pulse nightclub in Orlando and the murders at Mother Emanuel in Charleston; the fact that though Philando Castile had been killed by a police officer and died from his wounds, the officer was found not guilty; the terror wreaked on trans women of color; a teenage Muslim girl murdered while on the way home from mosque. These and other losses swirled amid the joy. In this prayer, I set up the both/and nature of the day—that we have much to celebrate and much to mourn and that God is present for all of it. I put us in the liminal space of a healing world that is not yet healed. People were deeply moved by the naming of the sorrow, grief, and other painful experiences and the strong affirmation of our community and our God.

Sometimes the language we use when we meet on the border is misunderstood or its meaning is contested. Let me illustrate. Middle Church worked on marriage equality at the New York state level and at the federal level. I was with members of my congregation and a sea of straight and queer people, celebrating at the historic Stonewall Inn, the day marriage equality became law in the United States of America. As I write this, I know that the word *queer* is both empowering to many LGBTQI people and offensive to others. Today, many of the young adults in my circles use the word to describe themselves; they eschew the LGBTQI designation that they might once have chosen and the labels the letters represent. Still, about four years ago, influenced by conversations both with young adults and in academic circles, I used the word *queer* for the first time in the pulpit, citing queer theology as a resource for my sermon. One man in his late thirties later told me he was deeply offended by this. He had been bullied for most of his life for being gay. I learned from my conversation with him that he would never accept this word, just as I will never accept the word *nigger*.

I tucked that word away and asked my staff to do the same. I dropped back, meeting with that young man and many other gay, lesbian, bisexual, and transgender people in my congregation. While meeting in one-on-ones, I was listening like an ethnographer for how they had described themselves at different points in their lives, for the language they used to describe their joys and sorrows, their feelings of marginalization and inclusion. I became a student, not just of the textbooks on my shelves, but of the living texts in my congregation. I expanded my vocabulary for prayers, sermons, e-blasts, and blogs by deepening my relationships with the people in my congregation. Though I am straight, I became a student of these cultures in such a way as to grow my competencies. And I learned how and when to use *queer* and when not to. Communicating God's revolutionary love to as many people as we can and honoring their cultures is a competency for leadership in multiracial, multicultural settings.

Consider another example, this one about the importance of communication as we organized Middle Church for the Black Lives Matter movement. Though we had been committed to being a multiracial, multicultural, intentional community for three decades, the context of our life together shifted around us. Across the country, the 2008 election of Barack Hussein Obama as president of the United States caused some to claim a post-racial reality and others to bring their racism and homophobia out of hiding. The onslaught of murders of black people at the hands of law enforcement reached epic proportions. From Michael Brown to Eric Garner to Tanisha Anderson to twelve-year-old Tamir Rice to seven-year-old Aiyana Stanley-Jones—black people lost their lives in encounters with police officers. Choked to death on a sidewalk; shot in the back; shot while sitting in an automobile; shot while sleeping on a sofa; shot while playing with a toy gun; shot while standing on a corner—their lives were cut short, and in too many cases to stomach, the police officers were not held accountable for these murders.

As Black Lives Matter gained prominence, some members of my congregation resisted. How can we say black lives matter? Don't we think all lives matter? These criticisms were voiced to some on the consistory (board) and to some of the staff. The leaders defended me, saying, "This is Jacqui's calling, and we must understand her particular passion." This did not satisfy me. To me, the Black Lives Matter movement was *our* calling as a congregation, not just mine; this call was a logical and theological extension of our call to be a multiracial, multicultural congregation, a manifestation of our call to be antiracist.

I took the criticism as an opportunity to teach. I realized that I was taking for granted that Middle Church understood the Black Lives Matter movement, that they were clear about why the movement existed and what it intended to do. I took for granted that my preaching provided enough background to bring them along with me. And I was wrong, so I dropped back. I took a little time off from preaching Black Lives Matter and did two things instead. First, I preached our vision. I reminded us of our identity and our history. I reminded us that we were the church that opened our arms to folks who were dying with HIV/AIDS, offering comfort, a hot meal, support, and spaces for grieving those who had died. I reminded us that while eleven o'clock is the most segregated hour for many congregations in the United States, it is not for us. I reminded us that we celebrate culture and heritage and ethnicity as part of our love of God and neighbor. I preached about our work on marriage equality, both at the state level and the national level. And I reminded us of why we march down Fifth Avenue every Pride Sunday.

Second, I supplemented what I was doing in worship and preaching with adult education conversations and with one-on-ones. I met with those who were most concerned (including my Chinese friend Gloria) to see what their questions were. Then we started a class called "Erasing Racism" in which we explored Scripture and read and discussed books to take racism on directly. This class flourished so much that folks who wanted to go deeper asked for more. So, we started a Healing Racism Task Force, a closed group of thirty-five people who would meet for a year to learn each other's stories and to talk about how racism impacts all of us.

With these classes as a context, I circled back to do some expository sermons on race. I came to understand that it was important to help Middle Church hear more than "Black Lives Matter" whenever those words were said. And so we began to speak of Black Lives Matter as the last phrase of a paragraph that went something like this:

> When black lives matter—when black children live as long as their white counterparts; when black mortality rates, HIV infection rates, and incarceration rates are more in line with statistics for white people; when the wealth gap between whites and blacks is reduced to zero; when voting rights are not eroded; when law enforcement officers are indicted for killing black people—then black lives will truly matter. Because black people are among the "least of these" in these United States, when black lives matter, all lives will matter.

Middle Church has been committed to being a multiracial, multicultural, fully inclusive congregation since 1985 under the leadership of my predecessor, Gordon Dragt. We work 365 days a year at the intersections of racial, economic, and gender/sexual orientation justice. As a womanist, I know that these issues are inextricably connected; these issues put us on multiple borders at the same time and require intentional communication. Middle Church holds in one space racial/ethnic diversity; genders/gender performance diversity; and sexual orientations. It is a brave space in which we also work to create safe-enough space for us to celebrate each other and wrestle at the places where wrestling should happen because we are different.

HEALING AND HUMANIZING THROUGH
WORSHIP AND THE ARTS

Creole-like identity can be formed only with intentionality in communities that are diverse in race/ethnicity, gender, sexuality, and class. Coming together is only the first step. Having brave conversations about these differences—communication on the border—helps not only to solidify identity but to prevent resentments and conflicts from growing unchecked. Celebrating the diversity is critical to the community valuing the diversity. Radical inclusion embraces the unique suffering and struggle of the community, building empathy and solidarity. Study in small groups—reading, participating in conversations, viewing films, and experiencing art—creates shared understanding and knowledge. Imaginative worship that features the arts creates a shared text that anchors the identity of the community. Worship and the arts also act as a source of healing in a congregation.

At Middle Church, we have five choirs. Here in New York City, it is quite common to have a paid, professional choir in a house of worship. With so many musicians seeking work, a weekly choir position is prized. Our Middle Church Choir has twelve paid singers. Three singers each on four parts, they are amazingly gifted sight-readers who rehearse for ninety minutes before worship and then stun us with the music they offer. Our choir is world class; many of them perform on Broadway and in classical concerts all around the country. They sing everything from Bach to the Beatles to Irving Berlin. They sing jazz and spirituals and anthems with such beauty. I have clergy colleagues who tell me they themselves don't worship when leading a service because they are working. Our choir makes me a better preacher, and—perhaps more important—it helps me worship! I like to sit right up front when the Middle Church Choir is singing; I can hear them breathe and feel the power of their voices flowing over me.

Our music team is working to get more people singing more genres of music as part of our call to create space for our racial/ethnic and cultural diversity as we worship. Our other choirs are composed of volunteers. The In-the-Middle Chorus sings about once a month and every Sunday in the summer. They have more classical taste and are supported by four paid section leaders. Our Middle Community Chorus was called into being by Emmy-nominated actor and singer Tituss Burgess.[3] They are young adults, many of them Tituss's students, who sing on Broadway and are aspiring to television careers. They are featured on the Middle Church album "Welcome!," which was written by Tituss.[4] The Village

Chorus for Children and Youth sings three to four times a year, helping us mark Children's Day in June,[5] Children's Sabbath in October,[6] and Christmas. In this remarkable group, the youngest singers have just learned to read, and the oldest singers are in high school. They are learning, through the music, about the power of song to change hearts and minds. They offer music from justice and peace movements, Broadway shows, and the world.

Our fifth choir is the Jerriese Johnson Gospel Choir, named for its founder, a charismatic African American actor who found his way to Middle Church in the late 1970s. A tall man with a big heart, Jerriese became an important part of the redeveloping church. Jerriese asked to start a community gospel choir, one people could drop in and participate in without signing up to join the church. He shared Gordon Dragt's "just as you are as you come through the door" welcoming spirit. Soon word spread in the East Village that Middle Church was a place where you could come, be loved, hear a meaningful sermon and music from two choirs, and then leave, ready for the week. Our all-volunteer gospel choir has grown to some forty singers—a rainbow of diversity: black, white, Latinx, and Asian, old and young, gay and straight. They are representative of the racial/ethnic and cultural diversity of Middle Church. And they can sing! Some are professionals, and most grew up singing in chorus. All of them give up two hours each Thursday night to learn music and pray with each other. They are our largest "small group."

At Middle Church, we believe all the arts are languages for worship. The arts speak directly to the heart. In our worship planning meetings, we dream of ways to punctuate the themes we are storying with art. One Easter morning, we put a tarp on the floor adjacent to the pulpit. One of our visual artists, Mary Jo, came to church dressed in coveralls with her oils, brushes, and a vision to paint worship. Beginning with the prelude, she painted the introit, the prayers, the hymns, and the sermon. We watched as her blank, white canvas turned into a cacophony of color. She painted the awe of the spirit we all felt. If your space doesn't lend itself to indoor painting, imagine taking worship to the streets, carrying beautifully painted panels while marching for justice.

Beside music, dance is the art we use most. Black shoes have tapped in our choir loft. Modern dancers have draped their bodies on our pews. Ballet dancers have balanced delicately on the pulpit chair. We have many choreographers in our community. Some have their own companies, like Kim Grier at Rod Rodgers Dance. Mark Dendy choreographs large pieces of work all over the nation. We have dancers from Alvin Ailey, Martha Graham, and The Dance Theater of Harlem. They are as diverse as my taste in dance. Ishmael Houston-Jones throws his body around in loose movements that seem unchoreographed but that are intricate works of art. Adrienne and Lutin are a couple who bring different schools of dance to shared pieces that they both choreograph and perform. Some of our dancers are actors who can dance, folks who used to dance, yoga practitioners who move a little, and people like me who took dance as a child and love to shake it to R&B. Some bring cultural and national (Japanese, Chinese) forms with them to the sanctuary. With this diverse collection of dancers and choreographers, we have surprised the congregation with dancers rising out of the pews, climbing to the tops of them, dancing in pairs down the aisles. We have danced with a large, silk, blue river on Earth Day. A couple and their children danced to Michael Jackson's "Man in the Mirror." And yes, classical ballet happens too!

When visitors worship with our congregation for the first time, they comment on how it feels to them like both a Broadway musical and therapy! We believe worship and the arts lift us up, preparing us for the rigor of activism and works of justice. We also believe arts drop us right into the vision of the reign of God on earth. Worship and the arts heal our souls so we can heal the world. Worship and the arts humanize the divine, bringing God all the way down to be with us. In other words, worship and the arts are incarnational; repeatedly, the Word of God is made flesh and makes a dwelling place in the midst of us. Worship rehearses the incarnation and the soon-coming reign of God.

REVOLUTIONARY LOVE IS A BOLD NEW THING

I had been at Middle Church for ten years when Trayvon Martin was killed. The murder of this young boy devastated us. I remember driving with my husband the evening Trayvon was killed, and John said, "Middle has to do something. We always do something."

"I know," I replied. "Do you have any ideas?"

John said, "What if we wear hoodies, in solidarity with Trayvon?"

I immediately called our media and outreach team. This was on a Friday evening. Our social media team created a special e-letter to say that we would all wear hoodies on Sunday in worship. Further, we asked that folk bring extra ones if they could, to share with those who were without hoodies. I arrived on Sunday to discover that even my classically trained director of music had purchased a hoodie from Abercrombie and Fitch! Hoodies in the choir loft, hoodies in every pew—we were in uniform, in our diversity, in solidarity with a boy who seemed dangerous because of his hoodie. Pictures of Middle Church members in our hoodies appeared in *The Washington Post* and *The New York Times*, and on MSNBC and CNN. One of our members wrote a song in honor of Trayvon, and our gospel choir learned and sang it. Trayvon's life gave us the opportunity to live out a new dimension of our identity. Not only were we intentionally multiracial and multicultural. Not only did we celebrate diversity as part of God's rich creation. We understood that we were also called to be antiracist as part of our life of faith. Standing up for Trayvon meant standing up for our values. It meant standing up for the rights of black people to live free of racism. When Michael Brown was killed, I was on vacation, and our staff did an excellent job of organizing our congregation that August. We prayed with our hands up, once again in solidarity, with the uprising in Ferguson and the young people who took to the streets to say enough is enough. Being a Creole-like community required us to be revolutionary.

When I returned from vacation in September, I found myself drawn into a movement for racial justice with colleagues all over the globe. We used the internet to teach and organize. Outraged by the choke-hold killing of Eric Garner and the non-indictment of the police officer who killed him, and haunted by his, "I can't breathe . . . ," we could hardly catch our own breath. Our nation was on fire over what seemed to be state-sanctioned killings of black people. Sandy Bland, Arlington Sterling—the list is so long. We marched and we "died-in" on the streets of New York, in our sanctuary, and in a cafeteria full of Washington-elected officials in our nation's capital. My preaching and teaching were revolutionary calls for justice. I do not pretend, though, that being a revolutionary is easy. Multiracial, multicultural work is difficult in a context of pervasive segregation, racism, and xenophobia. Worship that centers justice work might engender conflict. Congregational leaders need courage to lead their congregations to this transformational work.

At the same time as I warn of the difficulty of the work in a Creole-like community, I know this to be true: worship is one of the most powerful tools for community organizing available to a congregation. Our worship is spectacular—spiritually moving, rich with arts, and with many voices participating. Even spectacular worship is not likely to be newsworthy. But music, art, preaching, and prayers can transform hearts and minds; it can story for them the role God has commissioned for the individual and congregation in healing the world, a role that itself might on occasion be newsworthy.

Leading a congregation in transformational work requires openness to the Spirit and to the world around us. Although our worship team plans worship six months to a year in advance, we make space for breaking news to shift what we do. When events happen around the globe—natural disasters, tragic violence spawned by xenophobia, one more death at the hands of police, or events on the global political theater—our congregation expects worship leaders to say something about it and give them a way to do something about it. So, our worship, justice, and communications teams collaborate to (1) plan what we sometimes call an "ethical spectacle" to highlight the current issue in worship; (2) alert journalists of our plans and invite them to worship with us; and/or (3) prepare a video clip or photos and publish them in the internet and social media. Our decision to wear hoodies during worship before George Zimmerman was arrested and after he was acquitted for the killing of Trayvon Martin was mentioned in dozens of news stories across many major news outlets. Likewise, thousands of people saw our message of celebration when we performed a wedding for three gay couples during our morning worship to celebrate after the gay marriage bill passed in New York State in 2011. Three hundred people saw the wedding in worship, but almost five thousand people have seen the thirty-minute YouTube video.[7]

The message of revolutionary love must also live outside the worship space of a church building. Sometimes that means we must march. I have marched with the most amazing people I know, surrounded by a horde of others, in search of truth and justice. There is something very powerful about praying with your feet. We marched in New York City for Black Lives Matter more than once, and for justice for Michael Brown and Eric Garner. We marched for the rights of women in DC. We marched against gun violence in DC as well. We marched to give a moral agenda to Hillary Clinton and Donald Trump when they were running for president. We marched against Islamophobia. We marched in Selma for the fiftieth anniversary of Bloody Sunday, and we marched at Mother Emanuel in Charleston when nine souls were slain. We marched in horror at the murders at Pulse nightclub in Orlando. We marched for marriage equality. We marched to stop an assault on health care; some of us were arrested as we stood up for the rights of God's people to have affordable health care. There is a palpable power in the hum and din of people chanting, marching, talking, praying, and singing. Marching for a just cause is itself a deeply moving sermon.

Those marching in the streets are community organizers and activists. Like those leaders, effective leaders in multiracial, multicultural faith communities are required to possess not only the skills needed to organize their own congregation but also the ability to analyze issues, network with others, and organize the larger community on issues of social justice and the common good. Without active engagement with the community and a willingness to put oneself in the public square to advocate for those without a voice—the children, the poor, the hungry, and the left out—the witness of the faith community will be greatly diminished. This is especially true for diverse, Creole-like congregations, which serve as a model for every faith community by standing with others and their concerns when those concerns may not immediately impact them. Those of us leading these communities show up for each other. We march for Black Lives Matter, we sign petitions for the rights of Muslims, and we advocate for LGBTQI justice and inclusion. We know it matters to our members and our constituents, and it matters to our community that they see our congregation parading down Fifth Avenue in the Pride March. Multicultural, multiracial faith communities walk their talk of inclusion, equal rights, and justice for all.

In conclusion, at Middle Church we believe that one of the most potent solutions to the blatant racism and white supremacy in our nation is the creolization of communities and congregations. When we live together, worship together, experience art together, and pray and play together, we disrupt the fear and suspicion that are at the root of racism in the United States. When we create brave and safe spaces in which to have the difficult conversations that must happen to grow relationships and understanding, we subvert the hatred and prejudice that foster the myth of white supremacy. We believe that God chose to come to be with us in the body of a multiracial, Afro-Asiatic Jewish baby from Judea; that the Creole baby named Yeshua is both the inspiration for and the telos of the movement called Christianity. What is required to heal our nation of racism is no less than a love revolution that leads to the creolization of our congregations and our communities.

Notes

1. Many of the stories in this chapter were previously published in Jacqueline J. Lewis and John Janka, *The Pentecost Paradigm: 10 Strategies for Becoming a Multiracial Congregation* (Louisville: Westminster John Knox, 2018).

2. Desmond Tutu, *No Future without Forgiveness* (New York: Doubleday, 1999), 31.

3. Tituss Burgess stars in the television show *The Unbreakable Kimmy Schmidt*.

4. You can find that album on our website at MiddleChurch.org and at iTunes.

5. Children's Day is observed on the second Sunday in June in the United States and on other dates elsewhere to support children. See NationalChild rensDay.us.

6. Children's Sabbath is sponsored by the Children's Defense Fund the third weekend in October to unite communities of every religious tradition. See https://tinyurl.com/y7vdp267.

7. Links to all these stories can be found at MiddleChurch.org.

3.

Church at Antioch: Creolization of Leadership

CURTISS PAUL DEYOUNG

Followers of Jesus arrived in Antioch of Syria in the thirties CE, bringing with them a Pentecost vision and a Creole way of living out their faith in community (Acts 11:19). Antioch had a population of close to half a million people, making it the third largest urban center in the Roman Empire. The city was highly diverse culturally, with Arabs, Armenians, Cappadocians, Greeks, Jews, Parthians, Persians, Romans, and Syrians. Jews had lived there since the earliest days of the city's formation. The Jewish community represented one-seventh of the total population of Antioch by the time these disciples of Jesus arrived. With the diversity came ethnic and religious tensions. Riots and strife were common in places where various ethnic groups interacted. Mobs sometimes attacked Jews and set fire to their synagogues. One-third of the population was persons the Roman Empire had enslaved. Antioch was an ideal incubator for a Creole-like faith community.

A team of Greek-speaking Jewish Christians arrived and established a congregation. They first reached out to Jews (Acts 11:19). This was consistent with the first-century church's decolonizing and reconciling strategy as described in chapter 1. The New Testament model was one where a congregation was first established in oppressed Jewish communities. Then later privileged, dominant-culture Romans and Greeks were welcomed into the congregations. This happened in Antioch when some Cyrenean and Cypriot Jewish Christian leaders also preached to Greeks (11:20). It was in Antioch that followers of Jesus formed the first congregation mentioned in the New Testament that could be considered broadly Creole-like, inclusive of both Jews and Greeks. It is probable that the wider cultural mix of people in Antioch was eventually represented in the church. In contrast to communities that followed societal norms and consequently suffered from high ethnic tensions, members of the Antioch congregation lived out an inclusive fellowship. In "the many house-congregations of Antioch . . . Jews and Gentiles, living together in crowded city quarters, freely mixed."[1] Jews and gentiles (umbrella term for people of non-Jewish cultures) continued to embrace their cultures of origin but broke with certain cultural rules that typically would have inhibited their ability to live as one in community. When they ate and socialized together, Jewish Christians let go of an understanding that their ethnic-religious identity required separation from other ethnic groups to maintain cultural and ritual purity. Greeks embraced Jews as their social and religious equals, contrary to assumptions in Roman society, where it was believed that Jews were "a people born of servitude."[2]

The Jerusalem church sent Barnabas to Antioch to provide leadership and serve as a link with the mother church (11:24). Barnabas recruited Saul of Tarsus (later known as the apostle Paul) to join the leadership team (11:25–26). Three others also emerged as leaders: "Simeon, who was called Niger, Lucius of Cyrene, and Manean, a member of the court of Herod the ruler" (13:1). The Antioch congregation selected a diverse leadership team in the early stages of its formation. Both Paul and Barnabas were Jews raised outside of Palestine and immersed in Greek culture. Yet they were fluent in the traditions of Jerusalem. Saul spent his school years in Jerusalem under the watchful eye of the noted teacher Gamaliel. Both were multilingual, speaking at a minimum Aramaic, Hebrew, and Greek. Manean grew up in Palestine in the household of Herod Antipas, his stepbrother. This was the Herod who beheaded John the Baptist and interviewed Jesus during his trial. Antipas's nephew, Herod Agrippa, persecuted the church in Palestine even as his "uncle" Manean provided leadership for the church in Antioch. (Herod Agrippa killed James, one of the original twelve disciples.) Lucius of Cyrene came from North Africa, possibly one of the African Cyreneans who initially preached in Antioch. Simeon, called Niger (black), was a black African.

All five of the leaders were oppressed Jews, following the first-century model for congregational leadership.[3] There were no privileged Romans or Greeks on the leadership team. Other than what we can infer from their identities, the biblical writers do not give us information on how these five came to be equipped for a leadership role as challenging as developing a Creole-like faith community in the widely and wildly diverse city of Antioch. Twenty-first-century faith leaders face similar challenges in the rapidly changing metropolitan landscapes of today (and even in many suburban and rural locales). This chapter puts the five multicultural leaders at the church in Antioch in conversation with cultural competency scholarship and the creolization process to develop leaders who exhibit Creole outlooks and skills in today's world.

CRITICAL CULTURAL COMPETENCY

We could assume that the five leaders in Antioch were chosen because they exhibited cultural fluency and flexibility like we observe in Creole culture. At the very least they must have been interculturally competent. Intercultural educator Janet M. Bennett and sociologist Milton J. Bennett define intercultural competence as "the ability to communicate effectively in cross-cultural situations and to relate appropriately in a variety of cultural contexts."[4] Behavioral scientist Beth Applegate prefers the term "critical cultural competency." Her term "critical" adds to the Bennetts' definition the analysis of "systemic issues of privilege, power, and oppression and asks the question 'Toward what end?'"[5] Applegate's definition is similar to the description of the creolization process presented in chapter 1: a response to oppression and colonization that restores identity and engenders self-acceptance, heals and humanizes individuals and communities, and revolutionizes societies. Critical cultural competency is a good descriptor for the skills needed by the multicultural leadership team facing the colonial realities in Antioch, one of Rome's leading cities.

Applegate further argues that critical cultural competency is "a way of being, a way of viewing the world and showing up in all aspects of your life [with the ability] to hold and value multiple perspectives" and the necessary social change required to fully coexist.[6] In the desire for intercultural competency, a satisfaction with just the appearance of diversity can pre-empt authentic inclusion. Educator and Six Nations member Patricia St. Onge notes that organizations often seek "to fill particular slots with people of color; lesbian, gay, transgender, bisexual, and queer (LGTBQ) folk; or other historically marginalized group members. [Or] hire or elect people of color who are fully bicultural and comfortable navigating the dominant culture." She continues that organizations often believe that "there is little need to address the systems of oppression if enough of the faces in the front of the room look like the communities who are being oppressed."[7] This image-making is not creolization. Creolization is transformation and not limited to demographic representation or tokenism.

Critical cultural competency requires that leaders do "the hard work of opening the organization to be affirming and welcoming of multiple realities and working together as a whole community or organization to determine the points of oppression."[8] We can assume that the leaders of the Antioch church were more than just representative of the various cultures existent in the city. Rather they were doing the hard work of creolization and reconciliation that led to the Antiochian model of Pentecost community becoming the blueprint for the first-century church.

Milton Bennett created the Developmental Model of Intercultural Sensitivity (DMIS) to describe the characteristics and practices that demonstrate a person is culturally competent. Then he and intercultural educator Mitchell R. Hammer designed the Intercultural Development Inventory (IDI) for measuring cultural competency.[9] The DMIS is described this way:

> The set of distinctions that is appropriate to a particular culture is referred to as a *cultural worldview*. Individuals who have received largely monocultural socialization normally have access only to their own cultural worldview, so they are unable to construe (and thus are unable to experience) the difference between their own perception and that of people who are culturally different. The crux of the development of intercultural sensitivity is attaining the ability to construe (and thus to experience) cultural difference in more complex ways.[10]

Bennett identified six developmental stages of intercultural competency:

- Denial of cultural difference—one's own culture is experienced as the only one.

- Defense against cultural difference—one's own culture is experienced as the only viable and legitimate one.

- Minimization of cultural difference—one's own cultural worldview is experienced as universal.

- Acceptance of cultural difference—one's own culture is experienced as one of several, equally complex worldviews.

- Adaptation to cultural difference—one's experience of another culture expands one's ability to include relevant constructs from other cultural worldviews.

- Integration of cultural difference—one's experience of self is expanded to seamlessly include the movement in and out of different cultural worldviews.[11]

In this chapter we focus on the development of critical cultural competency for persons of color and those who do not hold dominant or privileged positions in society. In chapter 5, we will return to the DMIS and apply it to whites and other persons of privilege.

ADAPTATION TO CULTURAL DIFFERENCE

The five Antioch leaders were likely at the stage of adaptation or its further developed form, integration. These stages would also describe Creoles. In adaptation to difference one intentionally attempts to understand life from another cultural perspective. As one becomes more adept at shifting one's frame of reference, interacting with people of other cultures becomes easier and more natural. Though it becomes easier, it does not mean that the interactions are not fraught with challenges. In integration of difference one internalizes "more than one cultural worldview and, thus, has an identity that can move in and out of different cultural value frameworks."[12] Adaptation occurs with awareness and intention. Integration is the stage where one shifts from one cultural perspective to another effortlessly or without thought. Milton Bennett writes,

> People at the adaptation stage use knowledge about their own and others' cultures to intentionally shift into a different cultural frame of reference. That is, they can empathize or take another person's perspective in order to understand and be understood across cultural boundaries. Based on their ability to use alternative cultural interpretations, people in this stage can modify their behavior in ways that make it more appropriate to cultures other than their own. Another way to think about this is that people in adaptation have increased their repertoire of behavior—they have maintained the skills of operating in their own cultures while adding the ability to operate effectively in one or more cultures.[13]

The goal in cultural competency development is to move from rigid ways to flexible ways of perceiving, that is using "multiple frameworks, or schemas." Psychologists Leilani Endicott, Tonia Bock, and Darcia Narvaez speak of "an individual's intercultural schemas [as] a repertoire of frameworks regarding social beliefs, cultural values, expectations, and assumptions that the person can use to make sense of the intercultural events and relationships in [one's] environment. . . . The increase in breadth comes with exposure to new cultural frameworks."[14] Milton Bennett clarifies that adaptation is not assimilation, which "is the process of resocialization that seeks to replace one's original worldview with that of the host culture. Assimilation is 'substitutive.'" Rather, adaptation "is the process whereby one's worldview is expanded to include behavior and values appropriate to the host culture. It is 'additive,' not substitutive. . . . The assumed end result of adaptation is becoming a bicultural or multicultural person. Such a person has new aspects, but not at the cost of [one's] original socialization."[15]

Persons of color in white environments can know their own culture and that of dominant whites. They can code switch as needed to succeed in white contexts. While shifting in and out of dominant cultural frames of interpretation and behavior may seem necessary for survival, it is not necessarily healthy. One must be careful not to take on or integrate the negative attitudes and behaviors that can come with privileged or oppressor status. People of color can become very adept at shifting between their culture and dominant white culture. But if they can shift only between their culture of origin and dominant culture, they have not reached the stage of true adaptation. People who have been raised in biracial or bicultural families or neighborhoods can easily live in both cultures, because both operate as cultures of origin. But if they are not able to shift beyond the two primary cultures, they are not at the stage of adaptation. People also fall short of authentic adaptation if they hold negative stereotypes or narrow religious beliefs about some other cultural group, such as LGBTQ folks or of people of different faith traditions. Prejudice blocks one's ability to exhibit competency where religion or human sexuality shape the cultural context.

Adaptation begins with cognitive frame shifting—viewing life from a different cultural perspective. This is followed by behavioral code shifting—behaving in a way that is appropriate to another culture. Janet Bennett and Milton Bennett write, "This developmental approach to intercultural adaptation stresses that code shifting should not precede frame shifting. In other words, it is important for adapted behavior to emerge because it 'feels right,' not because 'that is how one is supposed to act.' . . . The major issue at [the adaptation stage] is, indeed, authenticity."[16] Educator Young Yun Kim notes that adaptation is

> an orientation towards self and others that is no longer rigidly defined by either the identity linked to the "home" culture or the identity of the host culture. . . . As an individual's cultural identity evolves toward intercultural identity, that person's definition of self and others becomes simultaneously less restricted by rigid cultural and social categories and more broadened and enriched by an increased ability to, at once, particularize and humanize [one's] perception of each [interaction].[17]

What Kim describes is consistent with the integration stage in Bennett's Developmental Model of Intercultural Sensitivity (DMIS).[18] In many ways what the DMIS calls integration is simply an advanced form of adaptation. At the integration stage, individuals have "internalized more than one cultural worldview into their own. Their identity includes but, more importantly, transcends the cultures of which they are a part. They see themselves as persons 'in process.' They define themselves as persons at the margin of cultures ('cultural marginals') and as facilitators of cultural transition."[19] Milton Bennett writes,

> People at the integration stage of development are attempting to reconcile the sometimes conflicting cultural frames that they have internalized. In the transition to this stage, some people become overwhelmed by the cultures they know and are disturbed that they can no longer identify with any one of them. But as they move into integration, people achieve an identity which allows them to see themselves as "interculturalists" or "multiculturalists" in addition to their national and ethnic backgrounds. They recognize that worldviews are collective constructs and that identity is itself a construction of consciousness.[20]

At the integration stage of the DMIS, one's cultural identity may not be anchored to any one culture. Some experience their "sense of self [as] stuck between cultures in a dysfunctional way." For those fully integrated in a healthy way, their identity is "defined on the margins of two or more cultures."[21] Interculturalist Margaret D. Pusch notes,

> The integrated person no longer identifies solely with one culture but is able to function between and among many cultures, having mastered the skills of bridging between them and enabling members of those cultures to constructively engage with each other, often for a particular purpose. . . . Having access to multiple worldviews, the integrated person is able to evaluate situations contextually, make ethical choices, and act in "the profoundly relativistic world." . . . Here is a person who is in a state of *dynamic inbetweeness*.[22]

MULTICULTURAL PERSONS

The hoped-for endpoint in the process of developing intercultural competency is to become multicultural persons. Or as Margaret Pusch describes the goal, to become persons in a state of "dynamic inbetweeness." For sociologist Peter S. Adler, a multicultural person is someone "whose essential identity is inclusive of different life patterns and who has psychologically and socially come to grips with a multiplicity of realities." He continues, "The multicultural person is intellectually and emotionally committed to the basic unity of all human beings while at the same time recognizing, legitimizing, accepting, and appreciating the differences that exist between people of different cultures."[23]

Adler identifies three primary characteristics that differentiate multi-cultural persons from individuals with a traditional cultural identity:

- First, multicultural persons are psychoculturally adaptive. They retain no clear boundaries between self and other personal and cultural contexts encountered. Their identity is structured on the intentional and accidental shifts in their life experience.

- Second, multicultural persons seem to undergo continual personal transitions. They are always in a process of developing into something different from what they were previously, while yet still grounded in their primary cultural reality.

- Third, multicultural persons maintain indefinite boundaries of the self. The limits of identity are not stable nor predictable. They are constantly open to change. Multicultural individuals are able to embrace major shifts in their frame of reference and have the unique ability to view their own culture of origin from an outsider's standpoint.[24]

The leaders in the Antioch church were multicultural persons, or in the process of becoming such. Margaret Pusch suggests what skills leaders need to develop to exhibit cultural competency. She notes, "While some may be born to be leaders in their own culture, leaders with an ability to deal constructively in intercultural situations are made."[25] Pusch notes five skills evident in leaders who are culturally competent:

1. Mindfulness—being aware of one's own ways of communication and one's process of interaction with others.

2. Cognitive flexibility—being able to create more cultural categories while resisting the temptation to place new information into old, rigid categories.

3. Tolerance for ambiguity—being nonanxious, even comfortable, in a situation that is not clear while discovering what is appropriate in new and culturally different situations.

4. Behavioral flexibility—being adaptable in one's own behavior when interacting with people from other cultural groups.

5. Cross-cultural empathy—being able to understand another person's experience through using one's imagination—conceiving of it intellectually and feeling it emotionally.[26]

According to Pusch, the fifth skill of developing empathy requires "a significant 'other-culture' experience."[27] Milton Bennett defines empathy as

> the imaginative intellectual and emotional participation in another person's experience [which leads to] a shift in perspective away from our own to an acknowledgement of the other person's different experience. This shift in perspective is often accompanied by a willingness to participate in the other person's experience, at least to the extent of behaving in ways appropriate to that experience.[28]

For Bennett, empathy is not just seeking to understand a culturally different mindset. Rather it requires active participation, enhanced experience, and changed perspective.[29] Mystic theologian Howard Thurman also spoke of using imagination to understand another person's perspective when he wrote about the spiritual discipline of reconciliation, "To send [one's] imagination forth to establish a point of focus in another [person's] spirit, and from that vantage point so to blend with the other's landscape that what [one] sees and feels is authentic—this is the great adventure in human relations."[30] Thurman adds that if one fully embraces this experience of another's perspective, "it is genuinely to be rocked to one's foundations."[31]

Patricia St. Onge suggests that what is required is intimacy rather than just empathy:

> I believe that one of the ways that we increase our capacity to work and live effectively across differences is by creating intimacy with people who are different from us. We do this by, not necessarily marrying or living with people whose life experiences are very different from our own, but by intentionally creating our lives in such a way that we have intimate relationships with a wide array of perspectives and life experiences.[32]

Cultural competency thrives when one's lived experience of empathy and intimacy includes contact with a wide diversity of people, thereby reinforcing one's journey toward multicultural personhood.

DEVELOPING CREOLE-LIKE LEADERS IN THE
TWENTY-FIRST CENTURY

As we consider how to develop Creole-like leaders in the twenty-first century, I welcome into conversation five women from communities of color and indigenous communities—Micky ScottBey Jones, Robyn Afrik, Sarah Thompson Nahar, Sindy Morales Garcia, and 'Iwalani Ka'ai—who are living out this Creole process in the United States. I invited them to provide an intentional contrast to the five male leaders in Antioch (Acts 13), but they also represent the rapid advance of women into leadership in this century. Women of color and women from indigenous communities are the vanguard of young activist leadership. From my vantage point, all five women represent a cultural hybridity that would be defined by the DMIS as adaptation or integration. Furthermore, they all demonstrate critical cultural competency that is Creole-like in both essence and practice. Our conversations began when they were each in their twenties and thirties. In chapter 4 they examine the Creole-like process that has formed their identity and leadership.[33] For now, I will introduce them and point to their origins. This lays the foundation for the processes of transformation they will describe.

Micky ScottBey Jones is an African American woman who spent her childhood in predominately white neighborhoods in Toledo, Ohio, and Knoxville, Tennessee. She attended black churches until her teen years. She reflects,

> I had worshipped primarily in whatever Black church my mother attended. My mother had two criteria for church outside of it being a Black church—that there wasn't too much hollering or noise from the pastor or congregation and that the services were short and to the point! So, as a child, I didn't have a deep, emotional, or spiritual connection to the Black church.

At age thirteen Micky became a Christian at a white Southern Baptist Church in Knoxville and began a journey through her teens, college, and marriage in predominately white evangelical Christian circles.

Micky describes her high school years as very focused on her conservative evangelical Christianity.

> I'd walk around the halls of my high school with my Bible and at least one other book from the Christian book store or church library. I attended two youth groups and two to three services on Sundays. I started Bible studies that met early on school days and shared the gospel (e.g., witnessing to friends with the step-by-step, this is how you "get saved" language) anytime

I saw an opportunity. I entered talent shows with dances to Christian music and followed strict rules about dating and sexual purity.

Even though she did not go to a Christian college, she "participated in several campus ministries and looked for a husband" at the university she did attend. Micky notes,

> I was involved in everything from campus Bible studies to the pop-up Christian "coffeehouse" in the cafeteria to the Baptist Student Union. I was also engaged by December of my freshman year—to a white, Southern Baptist–raised young man who I met through early encounters in the Christian music industry. He worked in Christian radio, and I soon became a back-up dancer for one of the few slightly mainstream R&B CCM (Contemporary Christian Music) artists.

Micky's faith was formed in a largely white, conservative, evangelical context.

> When I tell people how deeply indoctrinated I was into conservative Christianity, they are shocked. They don't expect someone like me to have ever had the beliefs I had. At one point I was a conservative, one-issue voting, homemaking, maybe-birth-control-is-wrong, creation-only-teaching, homeschooling-to-give-my-children-a-Christian-foundation mama. At the same time, most of the media I consumed, especially music, was about God, personal holiness, and eternal life. I listened to Christian music radio (mostly white but occasional Black gospel) and conservative talk radio, and was immersed in the culture and industry that provided this entertainment to others.

Robyn Afrik is a Korean-born adoptee who was raised by a Christian Reformed Church, white, Dutch family in Holland, Michigan. She reflects,

> I was adopted at six months of age and brought to this predominately white Dutch community of Holland. I would later read in a newspaper interview of my adopted parents, how they initially wanted to adopt domestically—this, by default, would mean an increased chance of Caucasian. Because the wait for children through international adoptions was far quicker and my adopted mother was in her later years, my parents were urged to consider international / transracial adoptions. Korea was a country that was pushing for quick adoptions at that time.

Robyn notes that her environment produced a colorblind life envelope for her. She states,

Being adopted into a white family, I think that on one level I knew growing up that I was not white. Whenever my parents would take us out into
the community, people would ask, "Are these your children?" And obviously they would say, "Oh yes, they were adopted from Korea." You kind of
knew from that point, you were different. But I'd get a follow up statement
to it, "Oh but you're not really different. You're just like us!" But no one
asked who the "us" was referring to. In that statement, there's a value being
implied: we see that you're brown, but we need to affirm that it doesn't
mean anything different from being white . . . US.

Robyn recounts how this same experience of colorblindness or honorary
whiteness played out in her life outside her family. She notes how children often did not employ a colorblind lens.

I was in an all-white school and little white children who didn't know better
would ask questions like, "Why do you look different? Why are your eyes
slanted?" And they'd laugh or giggle or point. Yet, no one ever asked them,
why is your skin white and why is your hair blonde or brown? Just the fact
that they were asking the questions, with a tone like "Why do you look different? Why do your eyes look different? Why is your skin brown?" held
a bit of a "What's wrong with you?" kind of attitude. It's almost like pro-
jecting a feeling that I was inferior.

This projection of colorblindness was also central to the faith community
where Robyn was raised. She states,

I grew up in a Christian home, Christian school, church, etc. God was
infused pretty dramatically in my understanding of race because of those
unspoken kinds of comments like, "We just don't really see your color. We
know that you're another color, but we're not going to acknowledge it anymore, because God obviously doesn't see color, neither do we." If I wasn't
brown and I was just like everyone else, they probably wouldn't have had to
say that. It would be understood. You don't walk into your house and say,
"Why are my walls white?" They just are. But you do say, "Why is there a
brown spot on my white wall?"

Sarah Thompson Nahar is biracial with an African American father and
a white mother. Sarah, like her mother, was raised in the white Mennonite community of Elkhart, Indiana. As a young child she and her brother
were acting out in a way that brought embarrassment to her mother.
Sarah recounts her mother's comment, "'Straighten up!' I remember her
saying. 'Remember, you are the only biracial children that many people will see. How you act will be how they assume all biracial children
act!'" She continues, "I internalized the truth and the excess of that state-

ment—people were often watching me for the reason of my peculiar racial identity, monitoring my behavior and extrapolating. I strove to let the world know that 'mixed kids' had something to offer. If I failed at something, I worried severely that I was letting down all mixed kids everywhere."

Sarah describes the context in which she was raised:

> The progressive Mennonite subculture I was a part of distinguished itself from the conservative Republican Indiana culture around it through various practices that expressed our religious values of simple living, pacifism, and equality among believers. But beyond these distinctive characteristics for which we strove, Mennonites of Swiss-German descent assimilated into the whiteness of northern Indiana. My church and community though did not often admit this or talk about it, nor seem to know what the historical weight of having white privilege meant, or how it impacted our theology and our understanding of our distinctives.

While Sarah was grateful for the depth of community care, the narrow confines of the Mennonite community also presented challenges.

> I attended the private Mennonite middle and high school which was down the road from the private Mennonite college. Though seventh through twelfth graders were not nearly as contained as in decades before, my experience was insular except for peace club, the service-learning experiences, and Martin Luther King Day presentations. What's more, the family pressure, internalized perfectionism, and a theology of a loving-but-rigid-God made for a tense and full secondary school experience. I was one of a handful of students of color in the whole school, all but one of us in multi-racial families.

Sindy Morales Garcia is a Guatemalan-born immigrant to the United States. Sindy states,

> As a Latina immigrant, my story does not start as the "other" in a new land. My story starts in Guatemala—the land of my ancestors—a beautiful and tangled tapestry of Indigenous, European, and African narratives known as Latin America. As a Latina immigrant in the United States, I was raised by parents who proudly and lovingly kept alive the culture, wisdom, and traditions of our people. From a young age I internalized an awareness that I am a continuation of a deep and rich communal narrative and its many shades of cultural identities. I learned to make sense of myself and the world around me by seeking the histories and cultural influences of those who came before.
>
> My *abuelito* Elfego and *abuelita* Angelica [paternal grandparents] lived in the mountain villages of Palestina de los Altos. My *abuelita* Eufemia

and *abuelo* Colixto [maternal grandparents] lived surrounded by palm trees and the tropical weather of Santa Rosa de Lima. My parents both became social workers, making their way to the middle of the country where they worked among the indigenous and mestizo communities of Chichicastenango. They met collaborating on a community project and married soon after. As the only two people in their family to marry someone from across the country rather than from a nearby village, my parents in their marriage wove together two very different cultural realities of our diverse country. My father was from a part of Guatemala known as *tierra fria* ["cold land/soil"], the land of cool and majestic mountains surrounded by pine-trees and indigenous communities. My mother was from *tierra caliente* ["hot land/soil"], the tropical lands near the Caribbean coast where the legacy of African slaves brought to the region centuries ago is reflected in the dark skin of her family. So it was in the mixing of warm and cold soil and their different cultures and histories that I was born.

Yet it was not long in Guatemala for Sindy. She shares,

The government's violent assaults on the communities we were a part of forced us to leave our motherland when I was five years old. Miraculously, we were able to get tourist visas into the United States. Pregnant with my sister, my mother and I arrived in Minnesota in the summer of 1992. My dad joined us a few months later. With violence behind us and uncertainty ahead of us, my mother courageously began a new chapter in our story. I still remember the tremendous culture shock of that day as we crossed into a new country. Gone were the lush green mountains that had framed my childhood and the villages and small towns that shaped my earliest years. It was the first time I remember noticing cultural difference and feeling out of place.

Upon arrival, Sindy's family "found a small community of Latinx immigrants in an Assemblies of God church, and a white family from the church welcomed us into their home as we got settled." Sindy reflects,

Although this family generously provided us a place to live, they did not invest in understanding us culturally so as to help us fully live and thrive. We also encountered a great deal of anti-immigrant hostility and racism, at times being treated as invasive species. Facing deportation after our visas quickly expired, my parents took the huge risk of applying for political asylum. Partnering with nonprofit immigration resources, they used their skills as community organizers to gather the needed evidence to make their case. And to everyone's complete shock, they won this uphill battle. A few years later we risked applying for permanent residency, remaining in a legal limbo until we were finally approved during my junior year of high school. I would not be granted citizenship until 2015.

'Iwalani Ka'ai is biracial, with a Native Hawaiian father and a white mother. She speaks of her origins:

> As a young child my 'ohana ["family"] moved to Mni Sota Makoce, Land Where the Waters Reflect the Clouds. It is the birthplace of the Dakota people. Unfortunately, war, exile, and mass immigration resulted in these indigenous lands becoming occupied predominantly by non-indigenous folks. Some of these immigrants are my relatives. It was here in Mni Sota [Minnesota] that I learned the meaning of family, began to discover who I was, and first felt the ramifications of being me. I grew up in a home where my ancestral roots were acknowledged, but the traditions were not pursued or developed. I was a brown child with wild curly hair, exotic heritage, bira-cial parents, and a name that no one could pronounce. If you didn't know, the Hawaiian population is small in Mni Sota. So it was a common occur-rence for my name to be incorrectly spelled and spoken. The butchering of my name had a deep impact on me. Deeper than I realized at the time. It's funny how something as arbitrary as taking attendance in class can become an exercise in exerting identity. It was simple: every time my name was mis-pronounced I was reminded that my heritage was different than my peers. That somehow, I was not the same as my friends. Beyond just physical differences, my name alluded to something deep inside me that was com-pletely unique—my blood, my ancestors, my heritage. Everything about me pointed to these relational ties that were so rarely discussed within my real life as a child. It was during these formative years that I first began yearn-ing for a home where my name would never be mispronounced again. At a young age, dreams of kulāiwi nei ["homeland"] began to take root in my heart as I longed for an island I didn't remember visiting.

'Iwalani further describes her heritage:

> I am what many folks in Hawai'i call hapa. I have the mixed blood of descendants who are Hawaiian, French, Norwegian, and much further back Swedish, Irish, and German. My father's name is Harold. He was born and raised in Hau'ula, O'ahu, by my Hawaiian grandparents, Stella Kamake'e'āina and Moses Ka'ai. My mother's name is Jennifer. She was born and raised in Roseville, Minnesota, by my Euro-American grandpar-ents Sharon Knutson and Robert Valois. For as far back as I can remember, I knew that I was Hawaiian and white. I knew that my parents had dif-ferent colored skin tones and got funny looks from other families now and then. I knew that they were raised in completely separate places and had different ways of speaking the same language. I knew that I had tan skin and a white mother, and at the same time my tan skin was whiter than my brown father's. I knew that my hair was dark and long and wavy when most my peers had straight or tightly curled hair. I knew all these things, but I still didn't know exactly what it meant to be me. I was constantly dealing with the tension of understanding myself as a whole versus the labels that

only spoke to fragments of my being. This tension only grew as I attended school and made friends with varying opinions and cultural backgrounds. As I grappled with my limited vocabulary and understanding of culture and ethnicity, I began to wonder why people always questioned and commented on who they believed I was. I thought to myself, how come people don't know what a Hawaiian, French, Norwegian looks like?

As we engage with the narratives of these five women in the next chapter, we must remember that developing cultural competency does not occur in a power-neutral world.[34] Persons of color, indigenous folks, and other marginalized persons must also navigate racism, classism, sexism, heterosexism, ableism, and other forms of bigotry and oppression. The reality of injustice and intersecting power differentials shapes one's cultural identity and determines how one responds to life's challenges. Therefore, the Creole metaphor is valuable for defining the process needed for developing critical culturally competent faith leaders. Creolization is a response to oppression and colonization that restores identity and engenders self-acceptance, heals and humanizes individuals and communities, and revolutionizes societies. It is not enough to see this as only a communal or social process, as in the case of Middle Collegiate Church (described in chapter 2). Each individual leader needs to be creolized. Simeon, Lucius, Manean, Barnabas, and Saul were creolized in Antioch as oppressed Jews who embraced Jesus's reconciliation process, which restored their identity as Jews and as humans created in the image of God. Their enhanced self-acceptance enabled them to initiate a healing process that humanized oppressed Jews, as well as privileged Greeks and Romans and revolutionized first century society. As we shall observe, Micky, Robyn, Sarah, Sindy, and 'Iwalani experience a similar process that transforms them into Creole-like leaders.

Notes

1. Richard A. Horsley and Neil Asher Silverman, *The Message and the Kingdom: How Jesus and Paul Ignited a Revolution and Transformed the Ancient World* (New York: Grosset/Putman, 1997), 142.

2. Neil Elliot, "The Apostle Paul and Empire," in *In the Shadow of Empire: Reclaiming the Bible as a History of Faithful Resistance*, ed. Richard A. Horsley (Louisville: Westminster John Knox, 2008), 102.

3. Allan Aubrey Boesak and Curtiss Paul DeYoung, *Radical Reconciliation: Beyond Political Pietism and Christian Quietism* (Maryknoll, NY: Orbis, 2012), 79–85.

4. Janet M. Bennett and Milton J. Bennett, "Developing Intercultural Sensitivity: An Integrative Approach to Global and Domestic Diversity," in *Handbook of Intercultural Training*, ed. Dan Landis, Janet M. Bennett, and Milton J. Bennett, 3rd ed. (Thousand Oaks, CA: Sage, 2004), 149.

5. Beth Applegate, "My Journey Is a Slow, Steady Awakening," in *Embracing Cultural Competency: A Roadmap for Nonprofit Capacity Builders*, ed. Patricia St. Onge (Saint Paul: Fieldstone Alliance, 2009), 24.

6. Applegate, "My Journey Is a Slow, Steady Awakening," 27, 28.

7. Patricia St. Onge, preface to St. Onge, *Embracing Cultural Competency*, xxiv.

8. St. Onge, preface to St. Onge, *Embracing Cultural Competency*, xxiv.

9. For DMIS see https://tinyurl.com/yc3yv94v. For IDI see https://tinyurl.com/yavsmw3t.

10. Mitchell R. Hammer, Milton J. Bennett, and Richard Wiseman, "Measuring Intercultural Sensitivity: The Intercultural Development Inventory," *International Journal of Intercultural Relations* 27 (2003): 423.

11. Hammer et al., "Measuring Intercultural Sensitivity," 424–25.

12. Leilani Endicott, Tonia Bock, and Darcia Narvaez, "Moral Reasoning, Intercultural Development, and Multicultural Experiences: Relations and Cognitive Underpinnings," *International Journal of Intercultural Relations* 27 (2003): 405.

13. Milton J. Bennett, "Intercultural Communication: A Current Perspective," in *Basic Concepts of Intercultural Communication*, ed. Milton J. Bennett (Boston: Intercultural Press, 1998), 28–29.

14. Endicott et al., "Moral Reasoning, Intercultural Development, and Multicultural Experiences," 407–8.

15. Bennett, "Intercultural Communication," 25.

16. Bennett and Bennett, "Developing Intercultural Sensitivity," 156.

17. Young Yun Kim, "Beyond Cultural Categories: Communication, Adaptation and Transformation," in *The Routledge Handbook of Language and Intercultural Communication*, ed. Jane Jackson (London: Routledge, 2012), 238.

18. The Bennett and Hammer Intercultural Development Inventory (IDI) does not measure for the integration stage.

19. R. Michael Paige, Melody Jacobs-Cassuto, Yelena A. Yershova, and Joan DeJaeghere, "Assessing Intercultural Sensitivity: An Empirical Analysis of the Hammer and Bennett Intercultural Development Inventory," *International Journal of Intercultural Relations* 27 (2003): 472.

20. Bennett, "Intercultural Communication," 29.

21. Bennett and Bennett, "Developing Intercultural Sensitivity," 157–58.

22. Margaret D. Pusch, "The Interculturally Competent Global Leader," in *The SAGE Handbook of Intercultural Competence*, ed. Darla K. Deardorff (Los Angeles: SAGE, 2009), 75.

23. Peter S. Adler, "Beyond Cultural Identity: Reflections on Multiculturalism," in Bennett, *Basic Concepts of Intercultural Communication*, 228–29.

24. Adler, "Beyond Cultural Identity," 234, 236.

25. Pusch, "Interculturally Competent Global Leader," 67.

26. Pusch, "Interculturally Competent Global Leader," 68–70.

27. Pusch, "Interculturally Competent Global Leader," 79.

28. Milton J. Bennett, "Overcoming the Golden Rule: Sympathy and Empathy," in Bennett, *Basic Concepts of Intercultural Communication*, 207–9.

29. Bennett, "Overcoming the Golden Rule," 207.

30. Howard Thurman, *Disciplines of the Spirit* (New York: Harper & Row, 1963), 125.

31. Thurman, *Disciplines of the Spirit*, 126.

32. Patricia St. Onge, "I Can Hear the Heartbeat of the Drum under the Surface of the Words We Speak," in St. Onge, *Embracing Cultural Competency*, 58.

33. All five women submitted their written journeys to the lead author, who edited their accounts for length and connection to subject of the book. Then all five approved of edits and submitted additional written material once having read the contributions of the others.

34. Kathryn Sorrells, *Intercultural Communication: Globalization and Social Justice*, 2nd ed. (Los Angeles: SAGE, 2016), 16–23, describes what Sorrells calls "intercultural praxis." This process offers another helpful approach for achieving critical cultural competency.

4.

Faith Community in the Twenty-First Century: Creolization of Women for Leadership

MICKY SCOTTBEY JONES, ROBYN AFRIK, SARAH THOMPSON NAHAR, SINDY MORALES GARCIA, AND 'IWALANI KA'AI

At the close of chapter 3 the journeys of the five women who have written this chapter—Micky ScottBey Jones, Robyn Afrik, Sarah Thompson Nahar, Sindy Morales Garcia, and 'Iwalani Ka'ai—Indigenous and persons of color who bear the marks of a creolization-like process, were introduced.[1] We have been formed as culturally hybrid persons with the capacity for adaptation.[2] Our racial and cultural identities are like that of a Creole, formed by cultural mixing due to colonization. In the French Caribbean, Creole culture is most often a cultural and racial mix of indigenous peoples, plus a restored blackness or African-ness, plus the remnants of decolonized European cultural fragments. The process of creolization is a response to oppression and colonization that restores identity and engenders self-acceptance, heals and humanizes individuals and communities, and revolutionizes societies. We now examine the creolization-like process that has shaped our identities.

RESPONDING TO OPPRESSION AND COLONIZATION

As women, Indigenous Hawaiian and persons of color, all five of us have experienced racism, sexism, injustice, and oppression. 'Iwalani Ka'ai echoes the warnings of the French Creole writers about the destructive power of colonialism and oppression:

> Everything I am, my DNA, my experiences, my thoughts, ancestral places, wisdom, and histories collide with a "historical" metanarrative based upon greed, conquest, power, enslavement, and genocide. I am shaped by this context in such profound ways that I cannot even grasp them all. That is the scary truth about colonialism: if the colonizer does their job adequately the colonized will eventually lose their language, spaces, and truths necessary to tell the difference.

Sindy Morales Garcia names oppression and injustice as what caused her family to leave Guatemala. And then to her surprise, she discovered an even more sophisticated form of colonial injustice in the United States.

> It was during my middle and high school years that the dominant narratives of patriarchal white supremacy and justified colonization caused the most confusion and anguish in my life. Success was regularly depicted as white, middle/upper class, and male. Most of my textbooks boasted of the glory of manifest destiny, painting the United States, Christianity, and capitalism as salvific blessings to the world.
>
> At times I was strongly grounded in the truth that my people are magic, drawing on the power of my family and ancestral stories. At other times, the poisonous muck of internalized white supremacy left me lost and confused. I often felt envious of my white friends' "successful" parents. There were many times I felt embarrassed by the way my parents stood out, believing the lie that their struggles and lack of familiarity with US systems were signs of their inherent inferiority. I shouldered tremendous pressures to assimilate; to exclusively accept particular manifestations of beauty, success, and intelligence; to internalize anti-black, anti-indigenous, anti-brown, and anti-immigrant stories as my own.

Robyn Afrik describes her adoption in a similar manner, as a form of colonization.

> As a Korean adoptee, I was taken from my land, culture, and people. I was given a new name, one that would be recognized by a people who cannot speak any language but their own. I would learn that my survival and dependence required that I assimilate, that I not question or desire the "roots" of my identity. These narratives, given permission by my white, Dutch American, midwestern Christian faith to run wild through my veins, are always reminding me how to remain quietly in my place. I learned my identity required that I be adopted twice—first, spiritually baptized in the lineage of a people who adopted me; then second, legally paid for by blood

with great sacrifice by Jesus and the American Veterans, who spoke different languages of freedom but were worshiped almost synonymously as one.

Sindy says her experience of oppression and growing awareness of the personal toll of injustice intensified even more during her university years.

> Although I had spent most of my life navigating predominantly white spaces, I was not prepared for the deeply rooted racism, sexism, xenophobia, and homophobia that I encountered when I found myself at an evangelical Christian liberal arts college. As a Pentecostal Latina immigrant raised by parents with labor jobs and socialist worldviews, I certainly did not fit the mold of the dominant culture. I faced a "one-size-fits-all" mentality that privileged the dominant culture and undermined efforts toward a more equitable and intercultural institution. I regularly encountered students, faculty, and staff with universalistic worldviews and theologies that minimized cultural differences and ignored historically constructed power dynamics. I was deeply disturbed by the popular delusion that being a "good Christian" meant being color blind. I twisted in anguish as the tremendous pressure to assimilate and toxic stress of constantly encountering racism took a physical, spiritual, and emotional toll that would take me years to recover from. Sadly, I was living an old and common story of institutional oppression. All the oppressed women within me were tired, and it would take all the ancestral power within me to keep going.

Robyn describes similar emotional, psychological, and spiritual consequences as she tried to navigate the very personally felt effects of injustice, microaggressions, and unconscious bias.

> There was a point in my ministry where my husband was like, "You gotta stop, because you're so bitter about it." And he was right. I got really angry. When I looked around, all I could see, smell, and taste was the injustice. It's like finally getting the aftertaste of oil in the water that you've been raised to drink as normal. When you have had the oil all by itself, suddenly you recognize the unconscious bias from miles away. You become so frustrated with the system, with the ignorance, with the way policies and procedures continue to play out the same old narratives that you start to get jagged inside. Faith, Bible verses—they can't stand on their own because they've been compromised too, and you can't speak up or else you become pegged as an angry Asian. But if you're too passive, you become part of the problem. It's terrible.

For 'Iwalani Ka'ai, she became acquainted with the history of injustice through study of the Jewish Holocaust and the African American civil rights movement.

This was my first lesson in systemic oppression and genocide. The depths of hatred, sorrow, strength, and resilience that I read about broke my heart. I wept for entire groups of people and a multitude of stolen generations. My heart cried out for answers and I made the choice in my spirit that I would stand up for people, that I would protect anyone that I could. I learned about the evil of apathy and the power behind one's lack of compassion. My ideas about oppression, resistance, identity, and justice expanded as I began to see the complexities of real life.

Then 'Iwalani discovered her own story as a Hawaiian in the history of injustice.

I will never forget the day I learned the in-depth history about the illegal overthrow of the Hawaiian monarchy and imprisonment of our Queen Lili'uokalani. My heart broke as I learned about the injustice done to our people. I was angry with God and for the first time, angry with nā kupuna ["elders/ancestors"]. As I sat there weeping, I cried out to my ancestors asking them why they didn't fight harder, asking them how they could let our inheritance be ripped away. As I sat there earnestly seeking answers, this was the response I got, "Ua mau ke ea o ka 'āina i ka pono ['The life and sovereignty of the land is perpetuated in righteousness']. We did fight, we just didn't fight like the hā'ole ['white person']." I was looking at this from a Western perspective. This is not the way my ancestors thought or lived. Ua mau ke ea o ka 'āina i ka pono. The life and sovereignty of the land is perpetuated in righteousness.

Like the others, Micky ScottBey Jones has experienced racism in her life and studied the broader history of injustice. But one event of traumatic racism affected her deeply.

After the death of Trayvon Martin in 2012, I was forever changed. Nothing could remain the same—not my mothering, not my relationships, not my faith. I needed more than *The Power of a Praying Wife*.[3] I needed a Christian faith that could actually handle my distress and confusion and loneliness of being a Black mother in a mostly white neighborhood who was terrified to send her babies outside in the same hoodies they wore the day before.

Micky awakened to her need to transform the daily reality of racism into activism and healing.

'Iwalani discovered in her ancestors' models of resistance a new resiliency for her own journey.

My ancestors believed in justice. They believed in goodness, faithfulness, responsibility, and aloha. They prayed, petitioned, educated themselves, and did everything they could. All because they believed wholeheartedly that since they had acted righteously, justice would prevail, and the monarchy would be restored. They were Hawaiian, they could not be anything else. As I continued researching Hawaiian history and culture I learned about mālama 'āina ["respect/care for land"], mana [one's "power or life energy"], and ka lāhui Hawai'i [a Native Hawaiian sovereignty initiative] in the same breath as blood quantum, colonization, and military bombing. The more I learned, the more complex my feelings became. I was angry, sorrowful, bitter, and proud all at the same time. The desire to see the Hawaiian people live and succeed grew stronger inside me. My faith in God was also changing in significant ways. All of these things were helping me define who I am.

RESTORING IDENTITY AND ENGENDERING SELF-ACCEPTANCE

To decolonize themselves, French Caribbean activists sought to rediscover what had been taken from them and their identity through colonization, slavery, and oppression. The first step was recovery of their blackness—a process they called Négritude. We have sought a similar kind of racial and cultural identity reconstruction. Sarah Thompson Nahar describes the push back she experienced when she began to reclaim her blackness.

When I would express the difference I felt—only once in a while would I dare—it was welcome as long as it was in the realm of aesthetics and "culture." But when my different perspective generated a critique of status-quo power dynamics, or injustice perpetuated by how systemic racism and classism showed up in the Mennonite community, it was often met with a response that conveyed a sense of betrayal. Responses from a white church member still haunt me, "Why do you feel the need to express your Blackness? Weren't we so good to you, and [didn't we] provide you with everything you wanted?" A list of the ways my community was kind to me would follow.

As a young person of African descent, I didn't have the words to respond or explain how difference itself was not the problem, but rather ongoing structural injustice in which we're complicit, no matter how "good" we are as individuals. I didn't know how to communicate that me pointing out how our community internalized and replicated some of the violence that our theology deplored was not to shame us, but to motivate us to greater self-examination as a part of our discipleship. So, I just shut down or sometimes exploded emotionally because I didn't have the word vehicles to interrogate the contradictions, the pressure, and mixed messages I felt swirled around my life.

'Iwalani describes how she felt that her identity had been erased.

> I remember being told once that "there are no racial slurs for Hawaiians because there are no more 'real' Hawaiians left." I stood there dumbfounded as I thought, *Do they not see me? I guess I don't exist, I guess my father was never born.* Dismissal is always an assault on identity, minimizing and erasing another's worth in one's eyes to justify according treatment. How is it possible for an indigenous place to no longer be considered native? How can the erasure of an entire people be considered destiny, desired, necessary for the common good?

It took an unsettling encounter with the Ku Klux Klan for Robyn to fully grasp the fact that she was not somehow racially white or at least an honorary white through adoption into a white family and white community.

> I went to a university in Indiana my freshman year and I made a lot of great friends who were still pretty white and normal for my world. We found out that the KKK was coming to rally on the courthouse steps. My girlfriends and I were like, "Wow, that's so wrong, anyone would know that. Let's go and protest." We grabbed our signs and ran out to the courthouse. We saw them handing out pamphlets on the steps to people. They weren't dressed in robes or anything, they were like normal white guys just standing there. One of the guys looked down to my friend on the left, and to my friend on the right, and completely just bypassed me. So of course, I'm thinking to myself, *They are the KKK right? They're supposed to ignore me.* But it just hit me—it was a backward paradox for me. The KKK chose *not* to acknowledge me based on the color of my skin, whereas my community chose to acknowledge me for the color that I wasn't—*white*—the one color they wanted to see.

When Micky began to move more intentionally to embrace her blackness, she faced a crisis in the faith of her upbringing and early adult years.

> I was wrestling with things that were bubbling up in the cultural landscape like the murder of Black boys in hoodies and middle-class families abandoning public school systems. So, I decided to go to seminary. I was already feeling like an ill-fitting puzzle piece in my church. I felt like we were speaking the same words in liturgy, with increasingly different spiritual understandings. I was the only person of color that attended regularly. I felt like the only one interested in a theological and spiritual response to various social crisis—Black Lives Matter, deportations, and more. The feeling, and at times choice, of isolation continued to grow. I felt largely unseen by and unable to connect with my pastoral staff and faith community as I became

increasingly vocal about race and the intersecting oppressions of life in the United States.

I chose the Master of Arts in Intercultural Studies degree program and co-learning community of the North American Institute of Indigenous Theological Studies (NAIITS) after a semester in a standard and ill-fitting distance MDiv program. One of the central themes of Indigenous theology has been discerning personally and theologically the question, "Can you be Indian and Christian?" Or in other words, what does it mean to be Indian and Christian? Can it even be done? The answer to this question has been answered *for* Indigenous people by papal order, various doctrines, residential schools, and scientific racism. Declared non-human or barely human, of course they were ineligible for salvation. So those who were not eliminated through brutal enslavement or genocide were civilized, that is, made white to be candidates for salvation. Civilization meant, of course, no Indian left—as it was said, "Kill the Indian, save the man." The task has been to reclaim and declare the Indigenous humanity that was stolen, including their spirituality, and build a culturally rich, relevant, and faithful Christianity honoring their innate connections with the Creator.

My question arose, "Can I be Black and Christian?" What does it mean for me as a Black person, a Black woman, to be a Christian? Can it even be done? As a woman whose people were forcibly brought here, given selected and manipulated Christianity as the only religion, and stripped of culture, language, knowledge, and spirituality, how do I not just react to the theologies of white men? But instead can I take back the fullness of my Blackness, affirming how it has been damaged, targeted, and stolen, and examine if it can co-exist with a robust, living, culturally rich, relevant, and faithful Christianity? Has too much damage been done to Black people, and to me personally as a Black woman, in the name of Christianity, for me to find value in the Scripture, traditions, and communities formed in the name of Jesus?

The efforts of reclaiming one's racial and cultural identity requires a context where that is possible. Sarah found such a place.

As I became acutely aware of my racial identity, I wanted to know what it would be like to be surrounded by other people of color instead of being one of the only ones. I was only what I called "theoretically Black." I wanted to learn what it was like to be a woman of color in this world. So, I went to Spelman, an all-women HBCU [Historically Black College and University] in Atlanta, Georgia. I hoped to fit in and have a chance to relax in my mixed identity as part of the rainbow of the African Diaspora. Well . . . it turns out your ethno-religious identity goes with you no matter where you are! I became an expert in explaining the differences between Mennonites and Amish (our buggy-driving, plain-dressing theological cousins).

The most jarring experience of realizing how my Mennonite theology had influenced culture happened in West African dance class. I was so happy to be in movement training and reclaim the embodied and beautiful part of my heritage that had been totally lost on Indiana Mennonites. Early in the class I could feel the rigidity in my shoulders, pelvis, and chest as the teacher invited us to isolate them; moving only one part at a time. I was not keeping on rhythm and felt totally lost! As I walked out of the classroom somewhat dejected, the teacher called after me, "What was going on back there?" I stammered, "I haven't been allowed to move my hips this way . . . I don't know how to . . . to . . . " I took a deep breath and blurted out, "Do you know what a Mennonite is?" She shook her head, bewildered, as she played out a pattern on the djembe. "Whatever religion or denomination that is, it has taken away your ability to dance!" From that day on I diligently studied African dance, asking my dormmates to teach me what they knew. I invited my body to relearn what it had lost.

Being in Atlanta for university significantly helped the development of my racial identity too. I was welcomed into the scene as a young woman of color who brought unique gifts and talents, just like everyone else. In Atlanta, I noticed that there were Black folks who were revolutionary, and Black folks who only wished to reform social systems. There were Black folks who wore their hair chemically pressed, and others who wore it in locks or an array of expressive natural styles. There were Black folks who were janitors, and Black folks who were CEOs. There were no restrictions on our freedom of expression and lifestyle choices. What a gift! There were Black folks and other people of color from all over the Diaspora who invited us to get to know the history of African peoples beyond African American. Being a Black woman of color was about being me and understanding my ties to particular histories of oppression and resistance—my belonging in a story of peoples who were now global but connected through (mostly traumatic) Diasporic experiences of loss of indigeneity and yet also survival and ingenuity.

Reclaiming her racial cultural identity was a painful experience for Robyn.

I didn't even know who I was. I started immersing myself with Korean students from Korea and international students. I didn't know who to talk to. I reached out to people who looked like me, who might understand this. I returned to Korea for the first time in 2004, making the Mecca journey back as an adult by myself, to the motherland. I came back weeks later to the United States, empty from a birth-mother search that lasted for years in my mind but took only a moment in passing. This feeling of disappointment and embarrassment brought a flashback of me standing in the grocery store line as a young girl, trying to explain to a beautiful, blonde-haired Dutch woman who I truly am because my adopted father doesn't look like me. She doesn't believe me; she wasn't bred to believe me, so she can't believe what she sees. After this debate, I don't know who to believe either. The Dutch woman's doubt starts chipping slowly away at the perfect picture I am given to protect myself from ever thinking I don't or can't belong to people like her.

And it's in those moments I begin reclaiming what it means to bring voice to being an Asian female in the world. Before I can even reconcile these things, I must give honor to a birth mother I haven't met yet. A woman I've made to sit quietly on the sidelines of my life. A woman I carry in my being—without trying. A woman I have hushed because I was too embarrassed of her face, her body, and hated myself. I will no longer do this—the struggles and truth of what I now voice are all in honor of her. They are a crying out to be found by truth.

'Iwalani rediscovered and reclaimed her Hawaiian identity by first finding a familiar home in Native America.

> When I learned more about the American Indian Movement, I began to question everything. It was a momentous season of political and cultural growth where I learned about intersecting identities, sovereignty, and seventh-generation sustainability. I began to actively seek out any Indigenous people I could find. It took me participating in every march and protest I was aware of to realize that I was already living in the heart of Indigenous territory. I attended powwows, gave prayer and tobacco as appropriate, learned to smudge, participated in talking circles, and walked the land. I found myself listening to Dakota and Anishinaabeg elders and feeling my heart connect to their stories as I found words for things I have always felt and known to be true. I am so grateful to the Dakota and Anishinaabeg people who embraced me during this period of my life. Learning about their culture awakened the deep longing within me for my own culture.
>
> When I moved to Hawai'i, everything changed. I struggled with understanding the differences between island versus mainland culture, local versus Hawaiian culture, and Christian versus worldly living. I up and left everything I knew for the birthplace of my father and found myself alone in a sea of relatives. I had to be completely independent in everything. I went everywhere alone and tried my hardest to get connected into my community. It was difficult, but I knew Hawai'i was where I needed to be. I got plugged into the Waimanalo Canoe Club, which became my first experience with feeling at home. I joined a papa me padauk ku'i 'ai class to make a traditional board and stone (for pounding kalo) and ended up getting connected to a ho'oponopono mentorship.

Creolization brings together and integrates all of who we are. As a Korean adoptee, Robyn has found this an important part of her journey.

> This is what I think or know myself to be. I may have cognitively known my birth parents are Korean. But I know myself to be Dutch, even though I look Korean. I think of myself as white, even though I am a minority. I attach to the thinking and reasoning of the majority around me, solving

problems and taking on attitudes that mimic more of the Dutch heritage than that of Korean. This causes much dissonance as I begin to wrestle with how I might learn to accept and love myself including others who look like me. But I am always reminded of my visual racial identity every time I consider the mirror. Simply, I am a brown skinned woman. I will never have a distorted view of this, as it is once again factual. I also honor my feeling racial identity. What is it I feel I am, regardless of other constructs, other imposing narratives or facts. What do I feel after all the noise has calmed down? I choose to identify with whatever that is, expressing and living it out.

As Sindy has sought to creolize her identity, she experienced challenge and rejection from others.

In the United States, race is often talked about as a black-and-white paradigm, lumping together or making invisible the many communities of color that don't fit into that limited binary. One of the most impactful classes I took in seminary was on womanist theology and ethics. As I encountered new narratives and reflected on my family's stories from a different perspective, my mother's story rose up in my mind and heart. Or better said, the lack of stories and oppressive silence around her blackness rose up. I felt womanism invite me into a new borderland, an edging and overlapping of the various cultures and lived realities of women of the African diaspora—a diaspora that reached the shores of Latin America and continues to live in the bodies and stories of women like my mother. Some of the African American women in my class took issue with the overlaps I was exploring, asserting that black women's lived realities must be respected and protected because they are constantly marginalized and made invisible by heteropatriarchy and white supremacy. Latinas should stick to their own spaces. I felt torn. While I in no way wanted to do harm by appropriating womanism, a million questions flooded my mind: How do we honor and protect the lived realities of Afro-Latinas? Is there such a thing as a *womanista*?[4] How can we honor those in our community with intersecting identities if our liberation work is rooted in frameworks of "either/or" and "us versus them" thinking? How do we cultivate open hearts and healthy boundaries that help us better understand and honor our intersections and particularities?

I felt that denying that the African diaspora has lived, loved, worked, and resisted in Latin America for generations could not be the solution. After all, Latin America is a crucible of complicated racial and cultural mixing. Ignoring my Guatemalan mother's African roots would continue to breathe life into white supremacy and colonization. We live in an interwoven world, and transformative, systemic change cannot be accomplished in silos. Just as no one community has a monopoly on divine revelation, no one identity group holds a complete analysis of power and oppression. To more fully understand and uproot the global and multi-armed systems of oppression that have strategically kept us divided throughout history, we need each other's stories, histories, wisdom, and insights. To co-create a life-giving world that works for us all, we need each other's imaginations, traditions of spiritually grounded resistance, and practices of unapologetic joy. I came to realize that we need to transform our cultural borderlands from a place of competitive and wounded hostility to a more fertile space where we can collectively thrive in the fullness of our multiple identities.

Micky believes her early years provided a foundation for her Creole-like identity.

I had friends of various denominations and traditions which is already an anomaly for many Christians—Catholic, Southern Baptist, charismatic, Lutheran, and nondenominational friends were all part of my coming-of-age story. I had Jewish friends whose parents included me in holiday celebrations and weekly services. I also had friends who were exploring their sexuality, some of whom now identify as gay—even though we didn't have the language for that as sheltered teenagers in the early and mid-1990s. Even though I became dedicated to a fairly conservative Southern Baptist and charismatic influenced faith in my early teen years, these influential interactions provided a base of appreciation for difference. In fact, they may have been the fissures in the foundation of my fundamentalism.

'Iwalani feels she reached a place of self-acceptance in her process of creolization and identity formation.

The development of my identity began in my learning who I was not so that I could learn who I was. When everything around you tries to squeeze the joy and ancestral histories out of you, leaving your bones bleached and exposed to the sun, you do everything you can just to survive. Part of surviving was choosing to love myself. To not fight myself and all the complexities and complications and cultural mixings that made me who I was. I had to choose whether I would be ashamed, proud, or accepting of the pieces of my identity in which the peoples and communities around me continuously chose to judge, categorize, and comment upon. I could either drown in the dissonance or understand my worth and define myself for who I really am. I am a strong Indigenous Christian woman. I am Hawaiian, French, and Norwegian. I have no doubt in who I am and whose I am. My ancestral heritage doesn't conflict with my faith, it breathes life into it.

HEALING AND HUMANIZING

The effects of long-term oppression on identity and the experience of repeated incidents of bias create a need for healing. Robyn speaks of her own self-hatred.

As I began to dislike my brown eyes, my black hair—I did it all in fear of being different. It indicates to others I don't belong as naturally as they do. And even though their questions remind me of these differences, it is also in the silence or the avoidance of such questions that the consciousness of such difference grows the loudest. As my embarrassment turns quietly to shame, I begin to get angry at a birth mother I haven't even met. A reflection of a woman giving me this brown color on my skin; a woman birthing me as a Korean girl; a woman I want to hide from others because she will give away who I really belong to. But I can't claim her any more than she can claim me or my adopted parents. I start hating a woman who has no voice.

I carry these things deep within me. It carves craters in my soul and with no voice to release, they leak out. What happened to me was a huge sword in the stomach, because I grew up believing in the lie that was told to me, that I was just the same as them. But I'm not white, and I'm not equal to them, according to white people. I wasn't given the right tools or education to handle these situations, especially to defend myself. I was not taught how to live outside of a community that wishes to remain color blind. Some of my "loss of trust" in the people that raised me came from the realization that this topic wasn't ever really talked about. It makes me wonder, *What is their love based on? Do they love me for who I am, or is it because of who I'm not? Do they love me because of how much I assimilate and keep their world happy and going?* I started questioning all those things.

Sindy echoes Robyn as she describes the devastating effects of her own journey through toxic environments of privilege and power.

I finished my time at the evangelical Christian university burned out by the burden of navigating a racist, sexist, and homophobic institution. Shaped by a strong worldview of individualism, it was difficult for many to understand my systemic critiques. I left feeling spiritually betrayed by their predominantly white patriarchal theology that denied the fullness of my humanity, as well as by sexism within my own Latinx spiritual community. I witnessed how Christianity continues to be warped to elevate and divinely justify the worldviews of the dominant culture in effort to protect and maintain their power and privilege.

'Iwalani had a similar experience.

At the end of my high school career I had an encounter with Jesus and became a Christian. My newfound faith led me to a private Christian university where every part of my identity was assaulted, sifted, and torn down. I was not prepared for the institutionalized racism, sexism, and xenophobia I experienced there. I had such a two-dimensional perspective of Christianity and Jesus at this point that the meek and submissive religion they taught in their church did not provide me with the true and necessary tools to bolster my faith through the toughest of these times.

Micky envisions what health looks like by integrating her embrace of blackness with fresh insights into her faith journey.

I have continued to ask myself what a culturally rich and relevant Black and Christian life and community can look like. I want to know what it looks like in my own practice as well. What does it mean to revive the traditions connected to the spiritual practice of enslaved and free Blacks who brilliantly hid their own worship traditions inside of the Christian practices they were forced to adopt? I continue to struggle with and experiment with what my Blackness and my reverence for Jesus means for an integrated faith practice.

When I went looking for theology to rebuild my faith after its unraveling, I had not only the frayed strings of the churches I had grown up with, I had Black theology, liberation theology, feminist, postcolonial, womanist, Indigenous, and queer theologies all bringing colorful strands with which I could choose from to weave together my evolving culturally particular faith journey and practice. I benefit from the faithfulness of the last two generations of non-white, queer, non-male theologians (outside of what is often just called "theology") who modeled what it was to wrestle with identity, culture, theological tradition, and praxis. When I found womanist theology, it was like coming home to myself. There was so much that resonated with where I was as a Black woman mothering young children and holding both the joys and pain of being everything I was and where I saw myself growing as liberation focused for all.

Sindy has also reimagined her faith in ways that have brought healing for herself and ways of humanizing others.

I would have left Christianity all together if it were not for black and Latinx liberation theologies I encountered that unapologetically denounced colonization, white supremacy, and sexism as structural sin. In these stories and theologies, I found healing for myself and my loved ones; I felt the presence of the divine in our shared narratives of struggle and resilience; and I understood the ministry of Jesus as a ministry of justice and liberation for the oppressed. I came to see that activism and my sense of calling toward healing and wholeness were one and the same. Spiritual practices and social justice work were not opposites but a part of the same breath and yearning for wholeness. I began to imagine my role in this world outside the frame of traditional ministry. My spirit also found much healing outside the traditional boundaries of Christianity as I experienced the divine in the stories of my ancestors, in the loving embrace of Guadalupe, in the gathering of women, in the life-giving arms of nature, and in the passionate pulse of community organizing. I found a tremendous amount of peace when I stopped working so hard to redeem the many problematic aspects of the Christianity I had grown up with, refusing to condone death-dealing theologies and oppressive biblical interpretation. My spirit finally felt free to encounter and embrace the divine in all of its diversity. While my spirituality has been shaped by my Christian upbringing, I no longer feel imprisoned by it.

Robyn recognizes that a process of healing is necessary to ensure that she will not allow herself to be hurt again.

I personally had to go through my own journey. I started enrolling in advocacy classes, institutes for healing racism, support groups for minorities. I started asking, "What is racism? Why am I feeling this way? And how can I get involved in stopping structural racism?" I started looking more closely at the marginalized in my community. "What are they going through, how are they going through these things?" I needed to understand by myself what happened to me and never to allow it to happen again.

Sarah sees healing as essential for sustaining activism.

I had a great professor who taught those of us in the activist collectives how to heal ourselves. She said it was crucial for feminists to know the herbal tinctures, the acupuncture points, massage techniques, and food medicine that we could always take with us for our ongoing balance, for two reasons. One, having heard the horror stories about the treatment of women of color in the patriarchal and white supremist medical establishment, we knew that the health care scene was a site of resistance as well—both getting access to it and good treatment within it are not givens. Two, we must feel the glimmers of liberation we seek in our bodies, to absorb the celebration of release of the internalized patriarchal and racist oppression—that will help us succeed in the long-haul struggles.

Sindy sums up the deep significance of healing as central to the creolization process.

My ability to cultivate my critical cultural competency has been greatly shaped by how much I have been able to prioritize and invest in my own healing as Guatemalteca immigrant. After surviving the violence of my university years, I realized that I was carrying ancient and intersecting wounds of colonization, racism, sexism, homophobia, and so forth. I desperately needed to disrupt and change the multigenerational story of trauma and oppression that I was ensnared in. I needed healing for my own story, for all the women who came before me, and all who would carry on our communal narrative after me. Not wanting to do the same harm that was done to me, I knew I needed to better understand and deconstruct my patterns of survival that undermine my ability to engage the cultural identities that

I have complicated histories with. We are not engaging each other with clean slates. We are the continuation of generations of complicated and violent engagements across cultural communities, and within our communities. To see beyond the distorting and disorienting haze of our trauma, we need physical and emotional healing, so we may fully know ourselves and see others as they truly are. It takes a village, and I slowly learned how to tap into all the sources of healing around me as I insisted on seeking out the wholeness my ancestors have always wanted for me.

REVOLUTIONIZING SOCIETIES

Creolization responds to oppression and injustice by restoring identity, engendering self-acceptance, and healing and humanizing people. Finally, the process of creolization revolutionizes societies and institutes justice and reconciliation. For Micky, working for social justice to transform society was tied to her faith journey.

> My theological formation and my social justice movement formation were concurrent. At the same time I was learning to exegete the Old Testament, I was learning the fundamentals of organizing in a faith-rooted context. I did not have to contextualize my movement work to my faith. Unlike others who learn Alinsky-style organizing and must learn how to combine it with faith practices or beliefs, I trained with nonviolent, direct-action elders and faith-rooted organizers from the beginning. While I had been an activist and facilitator in several contexts as a teenager and a young mother, I never saw it as activism or organizing and had no formal training. It wasn't until I started to understand that I was interested in justice precisely because stories of Jesus seemed to revolve around calling out, addressing, and righting injustice that I could see the through line in my community engagement that started as a teenager! I studied movement leaders from different times, and many of them were connected to faith—mine or another tradition—giving me inspiration that my obsession with making things right in the world was not an addendum to my faith but clearly central to it.

From a young age, Sindy engaged in truth telling, first warning her own community of the unjust realities of life in the United States. Then she spoke truth to the powers of injustice she faced to create space for revolutionary ways of being.

> As the first to learn English in my family, I became my family's translator and cultural interpreter as we navigated this new country. Following in the footsteps of many audacious women in my family, I became a truth teller as I learned to articulate the disruptive truth of our lived reality to the gatekeepers and powerholders of various institutions, systems, and communi-

ties. I was often met with impatience or hostility as I pointed out the cracks in policies or systems that we kept falling through. The message that we did not belong was often reinforced as we challenged the one-size-fits-all assumptions and approaches of the dominant culture. As a child negotiating with adults in service of my family, I carried a heavy sense of responsibility to help protect my family's dignity in dehumanizing situations. To survive and access what we needed, recognizing and naming cultural differences and power dynamics became a regular practice in my life. My young, brown body grew into adulthood holding the many conflicting feelings of a truth teller, at times feeling powerful and determined while also feeling terrified and anxious.

Revolutionizing societies and working for social justice are efforts that require intentional activism and organizing. Sarah describes such a moment where faith and healing joined hands with action.

It was early morning on my thirtieth birthday. I was in Geongjeong on Jeju Island, South Korea, at the invitation of the village leaders. They asked the international community to join them in their struggle to preserve the sacred site (especially rocks and minerals used for healing and water purification) on which the United States was creating a joint military base with South Korea to dock missile defense shields and stockpile weapons to accompany the West's "pivot towards Asia." Practitioners of Korean liberation theology (Minjung, Catholic, Buddhist) worked together to mobilize their faith in resistance to the harm and deceit perpetuated on the local people, who had voted against having a military base. They bowed in religious observance to block an entrance to the base so that the construction trucks could not enter. Police gathered but would not mess with people observing their religious practices. When the bows finished, the police threatened arrest.

After some hours, we were summoned again with the invitation to communion! When we arrived, I saw that Catholic mass was already in session. The Catholic priest walked to the gates of the military base and lifted the elements. The cranes and earth-movers were grinding away inside. *Boom! Boom! Boom!* A giant jackhammer was striking the sacred Gureombi rocks. "This is my body broken for you." The priest lifted the bread high in his hands, breaking it over the cup. *Boom! Boom! Boom!* The jackhammer continued. "And this is my blood, poured out for you for the forgiveness of sins!" He raised his voice to be heard, proclaiming the mystery of the Christian faith with all his might. "Every time you eat this bread and drink this cup, do it in remembrance of me."

I felt the vibrations of the nails going into Jesus's hands on the cross as the jackhammer pounded the earth. *The body of Earth is the body of Christ.* Earth is what is being crucified now. Since all life is interconnected, *the body of Christ is the body of the earth.* On cue, the congregation lined up. One by one, they stood on the road encircling the base to prevent any machinery, construction workers, or soldiers to enter or exit, or cars to pass while the sacrament occurred. Everyone moved slowly and deliberately, their taking of communion an act of incarnational defiance of evil, in this case manifesting in the form of militarism, ecological devastation, and corruption.

It has been experiences like this on Jeju Island that have helped me become culturally competent and to reach deep into the Source for the sustenance to face "the powers and principalities," oppression, and personal difficulties. To be alongside people with self-awareness, follow their local leadership, and struggling together for a healthy, sane world has formed and re-formed me. It has grounded any abstract theories I have, expanding my imagination about what is possible on this planet, while simultaneously reminding me of what is important in life.

Behind and in front of activism and structure change is the daily resistance of living one's Creole. 'Iwalani comments,

When someone thinks they have the right to change or degrade my identity with their unwanted sentiments, I can immediately respond with "That's not who I am" and "That is not who we are." When someone tells me there are no more Hawaiians or that my culture is dead, I can point them to events and programs and families who speak fluent 'ōlelo Hawai'i and talk story and do ho'oponopono and paddle and dance hula and pound kalo. I want to foster and enrich what exists. This is culture. It is not everything our ancestors were, but everything we are now. It means we honor our ancestors by sharing histories and practices and ways of speaking and being and living by making them pertinent and accessible and relevant now. It means making connections between old and new and giving words to feelings and experiences and ways of thinking.

A CREOLE-LIKE LEADER

We all reflect, live, and act as Creole-like leaders. For Sindy, Creole-like leadership expresses itself through leadership that is communal, contextual, and collaborative.

My parent's community-organizing work and the powerful women and men they collaborated with shaped my earliest memories and deeply internalized sense of communal leadership. From a young age I took on the role of caretaker, path-blazer, cultural bridge, and truth teller as I partnered with my parents to build a new life in this country. As the first to go through the education system in this country, I often had to navigate this new terrain on my own. I quickly became intimately familiar with the great vulnerability of having to ask adults outside my family for help. Fueled by the courageous brilliance of my parent's childhood stories, I longed to do my part to honor and continue my community's narrative of audacious courage and transformative resilience. I wanted to shove my foot in the back door and swing it wide open so that those I cared about could flood in, share, and influence new spaces with me and weave together our collective gifts and wisdom to build a better world. The communal leadership I witnessed as a child planted a seed deep within me that has grown into my current work of advancing racial equity by cultivating and supporting community-driven collaborations.

Reaching out across our different communities to create something together calls us to press into spaces of transformative ambiguity. This means stepping into uncertain and at-times unfamiliar ways of living, dreaming, loving, and working together. I have found that this requires a great deal of personal and communal reflection about the assumptions, worldviews, and values that shaped how we engage each other. I have learned the importance of paying attention to the various cultural layers that each person brings with them, as well as the organizational culture that shapes how people show up and work with each other. Learning to reject the myth of perfection and embrace vulnerability has nourished my life and work. I'm deeply grateful for my mentors who push me to constantly try something new and reflect on what I learn in the process. Learning to honor and love my inner child by intentionally cultivating a spirit of curiosity and playful learning has breathed new life into what I have dared to imagine and create.

Micky embodies Creole-like leadership at the intersections of faith, movement, and generation.

My entrepreneurial spirit always has me wondering what it means to forge my own path as a person of faith and leader and yet stay connected and accountable to my people(s). I am not ordained, as I did not grow up with a strong denominational tie within the Black church, and none of the denominations of my teen years or early adulthood would be a theological match anymore. I am not opposed to ordination, though, and continue to revisit it from time to time. I see it as less of a call (my call is to be a doula and healer in movement space) and more of a tool that can be used to leverage spiritual and cultural power to bring about shalom.

I have a creolized faith—in part of my own doing and in part because of my circumstances. I was formed in several different primary faith environments—the Black church and majority-white Southern Baptist and charismatic churches. I am a conservative evangelical turned progressive-faith-rooted, non-affiliated movement leader. I have volunteered in churches and worked in faith-based nonprofit organizations. I am a faith leader who has several different communities, and we opt-in to connection with each other. Another way that I straddle different worlds is generations. I am part Generation X and part Millennial. I had a pager and cassette tapes as a late teen yet have fully and easily converted to digital music and a phone that doubles as a computer that can fit in my pocket. I have made connections with other POC theologians, activists, and Christians on Twitter and Facebook who have become collaborators, coworkers, and friends. During the early days of Ferguson, Twitter and Facebook—especially those who were livestreaming or tweeting from the protests—were my lifelines. The intensity of conversations during those times, those leading up to that time, and the conversations that continue have been a part of creating community that is largely online but that occasionally meets in real time at conferences, events, and gatherings. Developing online community has also given me new energy, commitment, and even connections for developing hyperlocal community to practice personal and social transformation on both the small, local and large, national/international scale.

Sarah embraces a Creole-like leadership that is both personal and professional, theological and cultural, and local and global. For her, everything is connected and has returned her to the bio-region of her birth, in northern Indiana heavily populated by Mennonites.

This journey carried me to California . . . and back, to Jerusalem . . . and back, to leadership in a global grassroots organization on the frontlines of peacemaking in war zones . . . and back, through various configurations of romantic partnerships . . . and back. I learned to believe in God as a dynamic, non-anxious presence and wove throughout my experiences of deepening Anabaptist convictions and Black ecofeminist experiences. In every location I've focused on liberation theologies, studying how our social location and context influences our reading of the biblical text. So, choosing to go to seminary back again in my hometown, I wasn't in a bubble doing theological studies, but rather a part of community mobilizations for positive social change . . . "protestifying" in city halls and downtown streets. I saw the power of holistic, inclusive theology to bring people together across lines of difference to agitate for justice.

Yet with all these sincere feelings about my home space and home tradition, I wrestle with both restrictive interpretations of the biblical text and its self-proclaimed boundaries. What does it mean for me to be an adherent of an ancient Near Eastern indigenous practice that I received meditated to me through whiteness? It is primarily because of the global influence of Christian hegemony that I access the tradition in the way that I do. How can I know what is healthy to cultivate and worthy to share versus what is heteropatriarchal, capitalistic, ableist intrusion?

I hear the world calling for spiritual leadership from people of all walks of life who can participate as healers, ceremony holders, guides, prophets, and pastors in the many movements for social change. The clamor is increasing as the fear and fragmentation perpetuated by corporate technocrats multiplies. Some days I feel my calling is sharpening, coming into focus at times like when I train multi-faith clergy and community members in nonviolent direct action to address state violence or white nationalist agitation, or when

I work with natural builders to construct a waterless toilet system that will help complete the cycle of food justice. They're connected.

Everything is connected for the Creole-like leader. Examining the connections of life is the question to be lived. We embrace the complexity of our identities; its constant making and re-making weaves coherently with a path of faithfulness.

Notes

1. All five women submitted their written journeys to the lead author, Curtiss Paul DeYoung. These submissions were edited for length and connection to the subject of the book. Then all five approved of DeYoung's edits and submitted additional written material once having read the contributions of the others.

2. As defined by the Developmental Model of Intercultural Sensitivity (DMIS).

3. Stormie Omartian, *The Power of a Praying Wife* (Eugene, OR: Harvest House, 1997).

4. *Womanista* equals womanist plus mujerista, according to Teresa Delgado.

5.

A Well in Samaria: Creolization of Whites and Privileged Persons

CURTISS PAUL DEYOUNG

The Gospel of John states that Jesus "had to go through Samaria" (4:4). Samaria was that rare place in the Roman-occupied Palestinian territories where a colonized and oppressed Jew experienced some sense of privilege. More than seven hundred years prior to Jesus's entering Samaria, when the Assyrian Empire forcibly removed ancient Israelites into captivity, poor and working-class Hebrews had been left behind in the region. Upon their return to Palestine, many formerly exiled Jews claimed that the Hebrews living in Samaria had intermarried with their colonizers and altered the Judaism they claimed to practice. Samaritans were perceived as people of mixed ancestry with confused religious beliefs. They were despised and marginalized in Israelite society. Samaritans had a much different account of their own origins. They said Samaritans were descendants of the Patriarch Joseph and his African wife, whose offspring were the half tribes of Ephraim and Manasseh.[1] While most historians have since sided with the Samaritan version of history, bigotry against Samaritans was extreme at the time of Jesus. One rabbi even said, "He that eats the bread of the Samaritans is like one that eats the flesh of swine." They were believed to lack ritual purity. This notion was further advanced by the belief that the menstrual cycle of Samaritan women started when they were born. Therefore, they were considered inherently and always impure.[2]

Samaritan revolutionaries reacted against these years of bigotry by placing human bones in the sanctuary of the Jerusalem temple during Passover early in the first century, prior to Jesus's entrance into Samaria.[3] Prejudice and tensions were high. Yet the Gospel writer declared that

Jesus "had to go through Samaria." The King James Version of the Bible intensifies the resolve of Jesus in this verse, stating that Jesus "must needs" go through Samaria. Most Jews travelled around Samaria when commuting between Judea and Galilee. They avoided all contact with Samaria and the people who resided there. Although Jesus had the option of avoiding Samaritans, he chose to enter their land and, as we shall see, fully enter their cultural reality. Jesus stopped at Jacob's Well to rest in the heat of the day while on his journey through Samaria. A woman came to draw water as Jesus was sitting by the well. Jesus asked her for a drink, and a conversation ensued. The woman expressed shock that Jesus spoke to her and had asked for refreshment, as he was a Jew and she was a Samaritan woman. The author of the Gospel of John noted parenthetically, "Jews do not share things in common with Samaritans" (4:9). Their conversation soon moved on to religion (4:5–26).

A deeper look into their resulting dialogue reveals that Jesus had studied the culture and religion of the Samaritans. He knew that the Samaritan faith tradition anticipated a Messiah, called the *Taheb*, who would reveal truth.[4] When in the course of conversation Jesus asked the woman about her husband and she stated that she was not married, he revealed to her that she had previously been married five times and was living with a man who was not her husband (4:16–18). Jesus did not state this fact to shame her. By revealing the truth about her domestic situation, Jesus demonstrated to her that he was the Revealer (the *Taheb*), the Messiah. The Samaritan woman confirmed this when she stated to the people in her village, "Come see a man who told me everything I have ever done! He cannot be the Messiah, can he?" (4:29). The woman invited members of her community to join her in conversation with Jesus (4:30). Then the community welcomed Jesus to stay with them for a few days (4:40).

As a Jew in the first century, Jesus was a person of privilege in any relationship with a Samaritan. If Jesus had been looking for a Samaritan cross-cultural experience, he might have invited a Samaritan cultural expert to visit him in Galilee in the comfort of his own cultural environment. Rather, he headed right into the heart of Samaritan territory. Therefore, his experience of Samaritan culture occurred in the context of Samaritan rules and ways of life. As noted, Jesus had prepared for this encounter by studying the culture and religion prior to entering the context. And when he entered Samaria, he listened to Samaritan perspectives.

Jesus's conversation with a woman in Samaria serves as a starting point for a closer look at what is needed for whites, males, and other people of privilege to become like Creoles. A question first must be asked:

Is it even possible for people of privilege to become like Creoles? The leaders of the first-century church believed that privileged Romans and Greeks could be transformed. So they invited Romans and Greeks into house churches composed of and under the leadership of oppressed Jews. Again I ask, Can people of privilege become like Creoles? Jean Bernabé, Patrick Chamoiseau, and Raphaël Confiant in *Éloge de la Créolité / In Praise of Creoleness* point to the possibility for a Béké (white) to become a Creole. They write, "In literature, the now unanimous recognition of the poet Saint-John Perse by our people as one of the most prestigious sons of Guadeloupe—in spite of his belonging to the Béké [white] ethnoclass—is indeed an advance of Creoleness in Caribbean consciousness. It is delighting."[5]

Yet we must still pursue the question, Can white people become like Creoles? Why? Because the significant gap in cultural understanding and lived experience between whites and persons of color in the United States is one of the greatest challenges in the formation of truly reconciled, Creole-like faith communities. Persons of color often live and work in a world dominated by white cultural ways and know much about whites. Few whites have a lived experience, a deep knowledge, and a disciplined posture of listening that might result in their developing a nuanced understanding of other cultural perspectives and the experience of racism and oppression. In this chapter, the question is explored, Can whites and other people of privilege become like Creoles?

THE CHALLENGE FOR THE PRIVILEGED

This chapter opened with the example of Jesus entering Samaria as a person of privilege. Jesus was well positioned to understand Samaritan oppression. He lived the experience of oppression as a colonized Jewish subject of the Roman Empire. So, his perspective as an oppressed person allowed him to more easily enter the Samaritan reality, even though he held a privileged position while in Samaria. This is also true for persons experiencing various oppressions today (such as sexism, ageism, ableism, heterosexism, etc.). But most whites in the United States have very limited, if any, direct experience of being racially oppressed or listening to and learning from those who have experienced racism. This lack of direct experience of racism or prejudice creates a significant challenge for developing critical cultural competence and an analysis of socially constructed power. Later in his life, Martin Luther King Jr. came to the conclusion, "I guess I should have realized that few members of a race that has oppressed another race can understand or appreciate the deep groans and passionate yearnings of those that have been oppressed and still fewer have the vision to see that injustice must be rooted out by strong, persistent, and determined action."[6]

In chapter 3, cultural competency was discussed using the six stages in the Developmental Model of Intercultural Sensitivity (DMIS). Many whites in the United States are on the lower end of the scale. Researchers Mitchell R. Hammer, Milton J. Bennett, and Richard Wiseman note, "Individuals who have received largely monocultural socialization normally have access only to their own cultural worldview, so they are unable to construe (and thus are unable to experience) the difference between their own perception and that of people who are culturally different."[7] The first three stages in the DMIS are denial of cultural difference, defense against cultural difference, and minimization of cultural difference. Persons in denial experience their culture as the only real one. In other words, if you are white and dominant culture is based on whiteness, you believe that being white is the essence of human culture. Other cultural expressions are considered at best marginal but mostly as deformed. Defense against cultural difference is the view that one's own culture is the only viable culture. People at the defensive stage often feel like they are under attack by other cultural perspectives and need to defend the normativity or moral nature of their culture. They are troubled by cultural diversity and changing demographics. Often, they protest against diversity or emphasize whiteness (e.g., white nationalism).

Minimization is experiencing one's own cultural worldview as universal. Differences between cultures are minimized. One's own cultural framework is used to determine commonalities, which mask "a deeper awareness of privilege and may lead to an overestimation of one's own cultural sensitivity or competence."[8] The challenge is clear. Whites, males, and others with a privileged worldview who are in the minimization stage believe and behave as though their own way of being is universal and even preferred by others who are not white males. Sociologist Milton J. Bennett writes, "While eschewing power exercised through exploitation and denial of opportunity, people in minimization unquestioningly accept the dominant culture privileges built into institutions."[9] A minimization outlook assumes that assimilation into dominant culture is desired and even required. This perspective is widespread among whites in the United States and keeps dominant white culture norms and economic advantages securely in place.

On the other hand, some whites feel a lack of cultural identity. The primary purpose of the melting-pot process in the history of the United

States was for white European immigrants to discard their cultural identities and melt into one new race—the white American race. White European immigrants found their common identity in being "American."[10] They let go of their culture and language (if it was not English) and adopted a version of the culture of white Anglo-Saxon Protestants. The melting pot stripped these immigrants of their distinct European cultures and forced their assimilation into a homogenized, white, racial construct.

The premise of white domination was constructed on a belief in a biological race hierarchy, with "Caucasians" as superior. Caucasians were believed superior to Mongoloids, who were superior to Negroes by birth and genetic ancestry. The racial designation "Caucasian" is loaded with implications of white supremacy. The terms *Negroid* and *Mongoloid* have been dropped from common usage for many years now. Yet *Caucasian* remains in wide use. I contend this continued usage speaks to something deep within the cultural psyche of the United States and white supremacy. For our discussion of whites and cultural identity, "white" (or the racialized term "Caucasian") is a social construct designed to undergird domination and supremacy based on racial hierarchy and is flawed as a cultural category.

The late Native American educator and activist Richard Twiss, member of the Sicanju Lakota Oyate, once remarked to me that in his research he had concluded that the loss of culture created by adoption of the melting-pot image has led many whites to embrace materialism as their cultural construct.[11] White culture has become tied to the material aspects of the so-called American dream—shopping malls, life in the suburbs, and the like. For some whites, the process of racial and cultural identity formation leads to a negative identity. White equals *not* black. White equals racist. For whites who experience a lack of culture in whiteness or who view whiteness as bankrupt due to claims of white supremacy, there is a temptation to switch to, borrow from, or appropriate others' cultures.

In 2015, the world was introduced to Rachel Doležal, president of the NAACP in Spokane, Washington, and an instructor of Africana studies at Eastern Washington University. She had been living and presenting herself as a black woman until she was outed as having been born to white parents. Many blacks expressed outrage at this revelation, as they were "not afforded the privilege of a malleable identity."[12] In Rachel Doležal's autobiography, *In Full Color: Finding My Place in a Black and White World*, she writes,

> Yes, my biological parents were both white, but after a lifetime spent developing my true identity, I knew nothing about whiteness described who I was. . . . I identified as Black. I also hadn't been raised by Black parents in a Black community and understood how that might affect the perception of my Blackness. In fact, I grew up in a painfully white world, one I was happy to escape from when I left home for college, where my identity as a Black woman began to emerge.[13]

It is clear from her autobiography that she perceived the whiteness she was raised in as racist, dysfunctional, and fundamentalist. So, she changed her cultural classification and racial look. Doležal explains, "Black is the closest descriptive category that represents the essential essence of who I am. . . . I know from personal experience that our true selves consist of more than the color of our skin or the texture of our hair. It's the culture we choose to inhabit, the lives we choose to live, and the way we're perceived and treated by others."[14]

There are many critics of Doležal's choices. American studies professor Michael P. Jeffries summarizes the thoughts of some:

> Doležal's transformation shines a light on the social distance between blacks and whites, as well as her inability to address her own white privilege. Doležal chose a spectacular racial renovation over living her life as a white woman who not only loves black people, but understands that her love and commitment does not eradicate the white privilege about her background because cross-racial intimacy is a magical solution for racism. It isn't. The point is that it was more appealing to Doležal to completely reinvent herself and erase her history than to live in margins of whiteness. She was more comfortable appropriating black efforts to dismantle racism than acting as an ally.[15]

Historian Crystal A. deGregory points out,

> We cannot ignore the ways in which Doležal has privileged herself to blackness as a black studies professor who criticizes white privilege. Doležal could have worked as a white ally—*as a white ally*. She could've attended Howard [University] as a white ally, married her black ex-husband, be mother to her son, teach Africana studies, and yes, be president of her local NAACP chapter, as a white ally. But Doležal didn't want anyone questioning her privilege to speak on, of, and for blackness.[16]

Womanist writer Morgan Jerkins adds, "When black women look at Rachel Doležal, we see someone who used our skin and hair as a cloak. She never lived in a black woman's body, because if she did she'd know that to be like us is to always dwell in a place of war."[17]

I have some sympathy for Rachel Doležal. She found no integrity in whiteness as she knew and experienced it. Her white reality felt untenable to her. If honest, many social justice–aware whites would express a certain unease with their whiteness. We would love to find a way out of the implications and responsibility of whiteness. We are tempted like Doležal to be something else. We are embarrassed sometimes and angry other times. Do we really want to be black (or other race) to atone for our inherited racism or felt lack of real culture? Some try to reclaim aspects of their European cultures of origin to discover a cultural identity apart from or counter to a white racial identity. For recent European immigrants, this may offer some cultural comforts and a greater sense of identity. Some whites are a mixture of many different European originals. Which European culture should serve as the foundation for one's identity? The families of many whites have been in North America for several generations. Their European culture of origin may be a remnant of an idealized distant past. There is also the problem that many whites in the United States are descendants of colonizing or slave-trading nations such as England, the Netherlands, Spain, and Portugal. Their cultural roots would need to be decolonized. Any remnants of pre-colonial cultures could be over five hundred years old. Blacks have created African American cultures from multiple original African ethnic cultures and a shared history and struggle in North America. Similarly, perhaps whites can form a "white" European culture from healthy remnants of European cultures, the stories of white civil rights activists, antiracist analysis, and a deep redemptive spirituality.[18]

Or, can creolization re-culture and re-humanize whites? Can whites become like Creoles? Certainly, whites can and should participate in Creole-like communities at places like Middle Collegiate Church. But can their own personal cultural ways and social analysis be creolized? And if so, what would that process look like? Can whites become something *new*, a synthesis or hybrid of many races and cultures—like Creoles? As I have repeatedly noted, creolization is a response to oppression and colonization that restores identity and engenders self-acceptance, heals and humanizes individuals and communities, and revolutionizes societies. To use the language of the DMIS, does creolization offer whites a way to progress toward adaptation as multicultural persons who gain critical cultural competence? We now consider the process of creolization as it relates to whites and people with privilege.

IMMERSION INTO OPPRESSION THROUGH
THE AWFUL GRACE OF GOD

Creolization for whites requires immersion into oppression. Jesus entered Samaria. Greeks and Romans in the first century church entered the homes of oppressed Jews and learned firsthand the effects of marginalization from those who understood it best. The oppressed Jewish apostle Paul mentored privileged Greeks and Romans side by side with Jews he was developing into leadership (Col 4:7–17). Romans and Greeks were mentored for leadership with oppressed Jews as though they were Jews. Interculturalist Margaret D. Pusch states, "Becoming interculturally competent requires a significant 'other-culture' experience."[19] Whites need a close view of the realities of oppression to understand the effects of injustice on people of color and to learn how to analyze the power dynamics that produce forms of colonialism. As we shall see, the late Robert F. Kennedy called what he learned from his own experience with people in oppressed communities "wisdom [gained] through the awful grace of God."

I am writing this chapter fifty years after the assassination of Senator Robert F. Kennedy in June 1968. Raised in extremely elite white racial and economic privilege, Kennedy transformed himself into one of the most trusted political leaders among persons of color. This was best demonstrated in his pursuit of the presidency in 1968. While this has been documented from a historical and political perspective, limited attention has been given to how Kennedy acquired his cultural skills and analysis of power dynamics to became amazingly adept at understanding and engaging people who suffered injustice. Evidence of the trust Kennedy had engendered in black communities was observed on April 4, 1968, when he was on his way to make a campaign speech in an African American neighborhood of Indianapolis, Indiana. He was informed that Martin Luther King Jr. had been assassinated. The mayor and chief of police advised him to cancel his speech and not enter the black community. They feared a race riot. Kennedy's car continued without police escort.

When Robert Kennedy arrived for his speech, many in the crowd of a few thousand had not yet heard the news of King's assassination. Kennedy shared the news. Then he reflected on the meaning of the moment:

> For those of you who are black and are tempted to be filled with hatred and distrust at the injustice of such an act, against all white people, I can only

say that I feel in my own heart the same kind of feeling. I had a member of my family killed, but he was killed by a white man. But we have to make an effort in the United States, we have to make an effort to understand, to go beyond these rather difficult times. My favorite poet was Aeschylus. He wrote: "In our sleep, pain which cannot forget falls drop by drop upon the heart until, in our own despair, against our will, comes wisdom through the awful grace of God."[20]

Kennedy was witnessing to his own life journey of tragedy as a point of connection but also to his personal transformation through disciplined listening and intentional presence that created deep relationships in African American, Native American, Latinx, and other communities experiencing oppression. He gained wisdom through the awful grace of God.

Robert Kennedy's journey into the Samarias of the United States took a leap forward in May of 1963 while serving as the attorney general of the United States. He invited noted social critic James Baldwin to assemble a group of African Americans to speak honestly to him about issues of race and poverty in the United States. A group that included sociologists, psychologists, activists, and artists met with Kennedy at his apartment in New York City. The meeting began with Kennedy's own comments about the positive role of the government in matters of civil rights. Then a young Freedom Rider who had been brutalized and arrested several times exploded. Jerome Smith began by saying that he wanted to vomit just being in the same room with Robert Kennedy, who had done so little to support the freedom struggle of African Americans. Singer Lena Horne described what happened next. "This boy [Smith] just put it like it was. He communicated the plain, basic suffering of being a Negro. The primeval memory of everyone in the room went to work after that. . . . He took us back to the common dirt of our existence and rubbed our noses in it. . . . You could not encompass his anger, his fury, in a set of statistics."[21]

As Jerome Smith kept up his relentless verbal assault of Kennedy, the attorney general turned away from Smith and ignored him. This made the others in the room even angrier, and they also began to speak more bluntly. Playwright Lorraine Hansberry spoke. "Mr. Attorney General, you can take all those pious statements and stuff them up your ass."[22] As sociologist Michael Eric Dyson explains, "He had an encounter that felt as if he had stepped onto a fast-moving train of rage and grief."[23]

According to psychologist and educator Kenneth Clark, "Bobby became more silent and tense, and he sat immobile in the chair. He no longer continued to defend himself. He just sat, and you could see the tension and the pressure building in him." Clark reflected later that this was "the most intense, traumatic meeting in which I've ever taken part . . . the most unrestrained interchange among adults, head-to-head, no holds barred . . . the most dramatic experience I have ever had."[24] Kennedy biographer Konstantin Sidorenko sums up the meeting:

> It shook Robert Kennedy to the core of his beliefs. . . . It was the most important lesson any American public official had ever received on the anger and frustrations underlying segregation, poverty and the entire black experience. Most other prominent men might have walked out of the room quickly. Robert Kennedy stayed there until the meeting fizzled out three hours after it began. He was angry, hurt and disgusted with the entire process.[25]

Hansberry concluded, "He wanted a whole bunch of fancy Negroes to tell him he was great and that the Administration was doing a fine job. When we left the Kennedy's apartment I had a feeling of complete futility, and as we got on the elevator I wondered if there is any way to make the white people in this country understand."[26]

After a few days Robert Kennedy began to embrace the experience. About Freedom Rider Jerome Smith, he said, "I guess if I were in his shoes, if I had gone through what he's gone through, I might feel differently about this country."[27] Historian John R. Bohrer notes,

> Bobby didn't let his pride overtake the lesson he learned that day. Over the course of the next year, the word insult crept into his talks about civil rights. . . . The rage he encountered on Park Avenue that day was the product of continuous insult inflicted upon [blacks] by society. The insult was what mattered. The insult was all that mattered. Bobby came to understand that. And in the coming years, he would not make [black] leaders come to him on Park Avenue. In fact, he would go to them.[28]

Learning to understand life from the perspective of those who are oppressed or suffering is a painful affair. It is wisdom gained through the awful grace of God. The sacrifice of assumptions and a humility of spirit are required for transformation to occur.

Six months after his meeting with James Baldwin and friends, Robert Kennedy's brother, President John F. Kennedy, was killed. Through the deep pain of that tragedy, Kennedy's soul opened to the experience of others who knew suffering. This accelerated his own transformation. Paired with his religious faith, embracing the wisdom found in struggle formed the Robert F. Kennedy who was loved and trusted by so many by the end of his life. Konstantin Sidorenko writes, "Even at the most tragic moments, when he could have without fear of criticism drawn a measure of doubt, he remained a true believer in a universe held to order by an omniscient and loving god."[29]

In *The Last Campaign*, a narrative of Kennedy's last eighty-two days, historian Thurston Clarke summarizes Kennedy's immersion into oppression:

> He had become an advocate for Native Americans after visiting their forlorn reservations as a U.S. senator and discovering that their school libraries lacked books about Indian history and culture. He had become a hero to Chicano farmworkers after participating in hearings held by a Senate sub-committee on their attempts to form a union. He began championing the urban poor after tramping through tenements in Harlem and Bedford-Stuyvesant, questioning gang members in Harlem and meeting a young Puerto Rican girl whose face had been disfigured by rat bites. He became determined to improve the living conditions of migrant laborers after touring a camp outside Rochester, New York, where the workers and their families lived in an abandoned school bus lacking running water or toilets.[30]

This was wisdom found in the awful grace of God!

A transformational moment came in April 1967 when Kennedy visited the Mississippi Delta. He was shocked by the poverty he witnessed in Mississippi black communities. Kennedy asked the media to stay outside when he entered the shacks. This was not a photo opportunity or a chance for publicity. His campaign aide, Peter Edelman, and Marian Wright of the NAACP Legal Defense Fund entered with him. From their recollections Clarke writes,

> In a windowless shack reeking of mildew and urine he came upon a mother and six children. A malnourished two-year-old girl with a distended stomach lay sprawled on the floor, surrounded by roaches and playing listlessly with a grain of rice. He knelt down and began stroking her hair and murmuring, "Hello . . . Hi, baby . . ." Realizing that she was too weak with hunger to respond, he gathered her into his arms and began rocking and kissing her.[31]

Marian Wright remembered,

> He went into the dirtiest, poorest black homes, places with barely any floor, pot-bellied stoves the only thing; and he would sit with a baby who had open sores and whose belly was bloated from malnutrition, and he'd sit and touch and hold those babies. I wouldn't do that! I didn't do that! But he did. And I saw that compassion, and I saw that feeling, and I saw how he was learning.[32]

Clarke continues, "Moments later, a little boy toddled into the room. Kennedy sat next to him on a grimy bed. As he rubbed the boy's distended stomach tears streamed down his cheeks."[33] Biographer David Margolick writes that Peter Edelman "later said that the trip reflected 'that curious way that [Kennedy] had of learning': not from books or testimony, but by seeing."[34] According to Cesar Chavez, Kennedy had developed the ability to "see things through the eyes of the poor."[35]

In the first month of Robert Kennedy's campaign for president launched in March 1968, ten of the first seventy campaign stops were in Native American contexts. His aides considered this a waste of his time. Kennedy did not care what they thought. He was led by his values. One of those ten events was in the town of Calico on the Pine Ridge Reservation in South Dakota. There he met a ten-year-old Lakota named Christopher Pretty Boy. His parents had died a week earlier in a car accident. Kennedy met him in a single-room cabin where he was living with eight others. No press or aides were allowed to join him in this encounter with Christopher Pretty Boy "in a shack in Calico, one of the poorest communities on the poorest Indian Reservation in North America."[36] Clarke notes, "When Kennedy emerged from the cabin he was holding Pretty Boy by the hand. As they walked through Calico, he frequently leaned down to talk to the boy."[37]

Kennedy's day at Pine Ridge included several events. In a speech at a school, he declared that Pine Ridge was poor "because the white man has not kept his word."[38] Then he convened his Senate subcommittee on Indian education at a hall on the reservation. A crowd of over a thousand gathered. Clarke notes, "When Kennedy noticed tribal elders standing along a wall, he stopped the proceeding and insisted that chairs be found so they could sit in the front, a gesture that is still remembered on the reservation."[39] Kennedy's very personal engagements with Native Americans caused Lakota Sioux activist and historian Vine Deloria Jr. to write about Kennedy, "Spiritually, he was an Indian!"[40]

Kennedy also often entered Latinx spaces hosted and guided by his friends Cesar Chavez and Delores Huerta of the United Farm Workers union. Delores Huerta reflected that Kennedy "came to us and asked two questions . . . 'What do you want? And how can I help?' That's why we loved him."[41] Cesar Chavez said, "Robert Kennedy came to Delano when no one else came. . . . He approached us with love; as people, not subjects for study—as Anglos usually had done—as equals not as objects of curiosity."[42] This connection was most evident in March 1968. Inspired by Gandhi, Chavez was on a hunger fast to ensure protesters would stay nonviolent. Chavez invited Kennedy to join him in a Catholic mass to break his fast. Once again, Kennedy's staff saw no political value in this visit. When Kennedy arrived, thousands were there lining the road shouting "Bobby! Bobby! Bobby!" Chavez said the connection between Kennedy and the Latinx farm workers was "a phenomenon that can't be explained. . . . It's that line that you very seldom cross—I've never seen a politician cross that line and I don't think that I'll ever live to see another public figure (do so)."[43]

The Robert Kennedy campaigning for the Democratic nomination for president of the United States in 1968 was a very different person from the man at the meeting with James Baldwin. Bobby Kennedy had learned and changed, beginning with that 1963 meeting and continuing with numerous other opportunities to listen and learn with blacks, Native Americans, Latinx, and poor whites. Near the end of his life, while campaigning in Oakland, California, he scheduled a meeting with African American community leaders at Taylor Memorial Methodist Church in West Oakland. His campaign aide John Seigenthaler recalled the gathering as a "rough, gut-cutting meeting in which a handful of people stood up and blistered white society and him as a symbol of white society. He sat there and listened and took it, and answered their questions directly and bluntly."[44] Kennedy's reflections showed a seasoning of wisdom: "These people have a lot of hostility towards whites and lots of reasons for it. . . . They're just going to tell me off, over and over. I've been through these before, and you don't do anything. You listen and try to respond thoughtfully. But no matter how insulting they are, they're trying to communicate what's inside of them."[45] Later Kennedy said, "After all the abuse the blacks have taken through the centuries, whites are just going to have to let them get some of these feelings out if we are ever going to settle down to a decent relationship."[46]

Journalist Jules Witcover reflects, "He was aware that such meetings were a catharsis for the black militants, and from them he drew a clear awareness of the intensity of feeling in the black community, and a better understanding of it."[47] Speaking of such encounters, Michael Eric Dyson notes,

> The unvarnished, unfiltered truth got loose; the reality of black perception without blinders or shades became clear; the beautiful ugliness of our existence got vented without being dressed up and made presentable, or amenable, or acceptable, to white ears. . . . If he had learned anything from his brutal encounter with Baldwin, it was that, whether he wanted to or not, he had to listen to the unfiltered rage that tore at the hearts and minds of millions of [black people].[48]

Wisdom is found through the awful grace of God in real, deep, extended, and ongoing immersion into oppression. Immersion requires the setting aside of whiteness and privilege to listen and learn. It feels uncomfortable, exasperating, unfair, and even offensive. It is necessary.

IDENTITY THROUGH HEALED WHITENESS

I have discussed at length immersion into oppression using Robert F. Kennedy's journey as an example. The creolization of whites and people of privilege is not possible without embracing the wisdom that comes through the awful grace of God. There are no shortcuts to an extended and ongoing immersion into the realities of oppression. The purpose is not to become a white savior but to fully face what has resulted from centuries of white supremacy and other forces of domination and economic colonialism. The ability of whites to move forward is directly related to their engaging with these painful realities. Educator Ali Michael writes, "White people, having learned extensively about the realities of racism, and the ugly history of White supremacy in the U.S., 'immerse' themselves in trying to figure out how to be White in our society, and 'emerge' with a new relationship to Whiteness." Michael says the dilemma is "we cannot not be White. And we cannot undo what Whiteness has done."[49]

The historical transition in the United States from diverse European cultural identities to one overarching identity rooted in white supremacism was created out of the need to dominate indigenous peoples and people of color and to *not* be black. Educator Timothy J. Lensmire confirms this premise: "As white people, we used people of color to figure out who we were. We used, and continue to use, people of color to create ourselves as white Americans. . . . Most white people in the United States live segregated lives, spend time at home, at school, at work, at worship, with other white people. And yet people of color loom large in the creation of white selves."[50] A disengagement from this unhealthy and oppressive relationship that white people have with persons of color requires disrupting the ongoing creation of a white identity that uses people of color. This occurs when we face the truth about whiteness and immerse ourselves into the realities of the harmful oppression of people of color and indigenous people. James Baldwin observed, "White people in the country will have quite enough to do in learning how to accept and love themselves and each other, and when they have achieved this—which will not be tomorrow and may very well be never—the Negro problem will no longer exist, for it will no longer be needed."[51]

Sociologist Matthew W. Hughey writes about the idealized white racial identity being rooted in "hegemonic whiteness." Hughey uses sociologist Amanda Lewis's definition of hegemonic whiteness as "a shifting configuration of practices and meanings that occupy the dominant position in a particular racial formation and that successfully manage to occupy the empty space of 'normality' in our culture."[52] In other words, hegemonic whiteness means that white is the standard, the norm, what everything else is measured against. Whiteness is dominant and central. Whiteness is so ingrained and interwoven in society that we do not even recognize that it exercises such control. Whiteness is economically beneficial. Everyone else is other, exotic, or marginal. Hughey argues that "whites, by virtue of their membership in that racial category, are not immune to the pursuit of the white racial ideal. They are, simply put, 'white bound.'"[53] Being white bound produces "identity compulsions that simultaneously constrain and enable the formations of white racial identity, and thus, white action and order."[54] So the question becomes, Do whites want to remain "white bound" in hegemonic whiteness or do we want to embrace a new healed whiteness through a process of creolizing our identity, so we can rejoin the rest of the human family? The formation of a new white identity can result only as we welcome a healing process.

HEALING THROUGH A CRITICAL WHITE DOUBLE CONSCIOUSNESS

Creolization is a process that brings healing. Whites need healing. Sociologist Becky Thompson and literary critic Veronica T. Watson speak of "the trauma of whiteness."[55] They argue that "whiteness in the United States has been predicated on reinventing itself, of never looking back, of running from its own history, often under the guises of 'progress' and 'freedom.' . . . White people carry with them memories and experiences that tell them that something is desperately wrong, that racism is not natural or inevitable."[56] Immersion by whites into the troubling realities of racial injustice and oppression is the prelude to any hope of a healing process for whites. Typically, though, whites are not "present to feel the pain of brutalized bodies and psyches, and then act from that knowledge." Too often "white people deny, justify, and then reproduce the very violence that was the source of their own dis-ease, often leading to . . . the emotions of white racism."[57]

Educator Robin DiAngelo uses the term *white fragility* to describe the emotions of white racism. White fragility is a state in which even a minimum amount of racial stress becomes intolerable, triggering a range of defensive moves. These moves include outward display of emotions such as anger, fear, and guilt, and behaviors such as argumentation, silence, and leaving the stress-inducing situation. These behaviors, in turn, function to reinstate white racial equilibrium. Racial stress results from an interruption of what is racially familiar.[58]

These emotions of white fragility include "withdrawal, defensiveness, crying, arguing, minimizing, [and] ignoring." Living in a state of white fragility means that whites have not built "the cognitive or affective skills" or developed "the stamina that that would allow for constructive engagement across racial divides."[59] DiAngelo concludes, "If whites cannot engage with an exploration of alternate racial perspectives, they can only reinscribe white perspectives as universal."[60] White fragility and the unrecognized trauma at the heart of whiteness may account for

why people of color often say they are not able to "get anywhere" with white people in terms of having reasonable discussions about race. . . . For people of color, it is unfathomable that white people do not know themselves and the world they have created well enough to engage these questions. But when one is chronically traumatized, much of life is lived in the land of hypersensitivity, if not outright delusion.[61]

Becky Thompson and Veronica Watson go further and name "dissociation" as one of the symptoms of trauma most evident among whites in the United States. They cut off themselves from the internal experience to protect themselves from and avoid "sensations and emotions that could be overwhelming." This kind of dissociation has infected white cultural norms and lifestyles. White people in positions of power "have so separated themselves from reality that they cannot see their own entitlement even as they are benefitting from it." Even whites trying to address and undo racism can still experience dissociation. Thompson and Watson warn, "Sustained dissociation among white people is evident when racist ideology is repeatedly performed to the point where racism becomes seemingly 'automatic,' inescapable, and/or justified. This is the shift where whiteness, and the trauma associated with it, becomes hegemonic."[62]

Creolization promises healing. In chapter 1, literary critic Wilson Harris called creolization "a saving nemesis" for persons facing various forms of oppression.[63] Thompson and Watson suggest that creolization can also be a saving nemesis for whites as the "dynamics of oppression (in this case, racial oppression) carry within them the seeds for their own transformation. Neuroses can be turned into resistance."[64] They build on W. E. B. Du Bois's concept of black double consciousness.[65] Du Bois used the term to describe the tension one felt when two or more competing identities were in conflict with each other—in his case a black identity and US identity. Blacks must develop an awareness of how white US society viewed them in contrast to how they viewed themselves. Thompson and Watson use the term *critical white double consciousness* to conceive of a remedy or saving nemesis emerging from the trauma of whiteness. This critical white double consciousness "is a spirit of atonement that seeks to acknowledge and recover that which has been lost to whiteness through violence and oppression." Critical white double consciousness redeems, saves, and heals white people by:

- Demanding a more complete and multivoiced narrative of the past and present, which creates honest self-reflection and accountability.

- Seeking out multiracial, multicultural interactions as an antidote to the one-dimensional narratives of whiteness.

- Learning the twin disciplines of silence and close listening as antiracist praxis.

- Committing to remain a fully present and vocal witness in the face of white lies, denial, and aggression.

- Retooling liability and trauma into assets for coalition building and organizing across race and other socially constructed differences.

- Nurturing spaces that make the personal and social transformation of whiteness possible.[66]

Living and leading with a critical white double consciousness means that whites are cognizant of the structural reality of privilege and hegemonic whiteness, while simultaneously envisioning and pursuing a healed whiteness.

REVOLUTION THROUGH CREOLIZING WHITENESS

In 1965, Robert F. Kennedy declared,

A revolution is now in progress. It is a revolution for individual dignity . . . for economic freedom . . . for social reform and political freedom, for internal justice and international independence. . . . This revolution is directed at us—against the one-third of the world that diets while others starve; against a nation that buys eight million new cars a year while most of the world goes without shoes.[67]

As Kennedy knew over fifty years ago, the revolution must be against structures of whiteness and privilege if we are to arrive in a Creole future. Becky Thompson and Veronica Watson add, "White people wanting to do antiracist work must come to understand that this commitment is essentially about saving their own souls [and] is essential to developing a white racial identity that is not based on subjugation and alienation."[68] There is room for whites in the struggle for a new Creole-like society. But first we must fully step into and be thoroughly transformed by a creolization-like process. Robert Kennedy did not live long enough for that process to be complete in his own life. In chapter 6, I put my story of sixty years under a creolization analysis.

Notes

1. T. H. Gaster, "Samaritans," in *The Interpreter's Dictionary of the Bible*, vol. 4, ed. George Arthur Buttrick (Nashville: Abingdon, 1969), 190–92; Joachim Jeremias, *Jerusalem in the Time of Jesus* (Philadelphia: Fortress, 1969), 355.

2. Jeremias, *Jerusalem in the Time of Jesus*, 357.

3. Jeremias, *Jerusalem in the Time of Jesus*, 353.

4. George R. Beasley-Murray, *Word Biblical Commentary*, vol. 36 (Waco: Word, 1987), 62–63.

5. Jean Bernabé, Patrick Chamoiseau, and Raphaël Confiant, *Éloge de la Créolité / In Praise of Creoleness*, Édition Bilingue (Paris: Gallimard, 1993), 90–91.

6. Martin Luther King Jr., *I Have a Dream: Writings and Speeches That Changed the World*, ed. James M. Washington (San Francisco: HarperCollins, 1992), 95.

7. Mitchell R. Hammer, Milton J. Bennett, and Richard Wiseman, "Measuring Intercultural Sensitivity: The Intercultural Development Inventory," in *International Journal of Intercultural Relations* 27 (2003): 423.

8. Mitchell R. Hammer, "The Intercultural Development Inventory (IDI): An Approach for Assessing and Building Intercultural Competence," in *Contemporary Leadership and Intercultural Competence: Understanding and Utilizing Cultural Diversity to Build Successful Organizations*, ed. M. A. Moodian (Thousand Oaks, CA: SAGE, 2008), 250.

9. Milton J. Bennett, "Intercultural Communication: A Current Perspective,"

in *Basic Concepts of Intercultural Communication: Selected Readings*, ed. Milton J. Bennett (Boston: Intercultural Press, 1998), 28.

10. Even the term *American* is often meant to be synonymous with citizens of the United States rather than inclusive of Canada, Mexico, and countries in Central and South America. Therefore, when used this way, *American* carries with it a sense of exclusivism and exceptionalism.

11. Richard Twiss, conversation with the author in October 2012.

12. Morgan Jerkins, *This Will Be My Undoing: Living at the Intersection of Black, Female, and Feminist in (White) America* (New York: Harper Perennial, 2018), 44.

13. Rachel Doležal, *In Full Color: Finding My Place in a Black and White World* (Dallas: BenBella, 2017), 1–2.

14. Doležal, *In Full Color*, 271.

15. Michael P. Jeffries, "Rachel Doležal: A Lesson in How Racism Works," *Boston Globe*, June 13, 2015, https://tinyurl.com/pd5m6j4.

16. Crystal A. deGregory, "HBCUs Ain't Handing Out Black Cards: Howard's Rachel Dolezal + Faux-Blackness," *hbcustory*, June 13, 2015, https://tinyurl.com/y79aqc9z.

17. Jerkins, *This Will Be My Undoing*, 51.

18. Civil rights activist Dr. Ruby Sales suggested this possibility to me. She thought it might be possible for whites to engage a process similar to blacks whose African cultures were partially stripped from them, usually losing the particularities of a nation, ethnicity, and/or tribe. She also suggested that this must be a spiritual process and should be pursued from that perspective. Phone conversation between the author and Ruby Sales, May 26, 2018.

19. Margaret D. Pusch, "The Interculturally Competent Global Leader," in *SAGE Handbook of Intercultural Competence*, ed. Darla K. Deardorff (Los Angeles: SAGE, 2009), 79.

20. Evan Thomas, *Robert Kennedy: His Life* (New York: Simon & Schuster, 2000), 366–67. See original quote, which Kennedy had memorized, in Edith Hamilton, *The Greek Way* (New York: W. W. Norton, 1942), 82.

21. Konstantin Sidorenko, *Robert F. Kennedy: A Spiritual Biography* (New York: Crossroad, 2000), 158.

22. David Margolick, *The Promise and the Dream: The Untold Story of Martin Luther King, Jr. and Robert F. Kennedy* (New York: Rosetta, 2018), 155.

23. Michael Eric Dyson, *What Truth Sounds Like: RFK, James Baldwin, and Our Unfinished Conversation about Race in America* (New York: St. Martin's, 2018), 9.

24. Sidorenko, *Robert F. Kennedy*, 156, 158.

25. Sidorenko, *Robert F. Kennedy*, 156, 158–59.

26. Margolick, *Promise and the Dream*, 156.

27. Margolick, *Promise and the Dream*, 160.

28. John R. Bohrer, *The Revolution of Robert Kennedy: From Power to Protest after JFK* (New York: Bloomsbury, 2017), 55.

29. Sidorenko, *Robert F. Kennedy*, 15.

30. Thurston Clarke, *The Last Campaign: Robert F. Kennedy and 82 Days That Inspired America* (New York: Henry Holt, 2008), 78.

31. Clarke, *Last Campaign*, 79.

32. Margolick, *Promise and the Dream*, 289.

33. Clarke, *Last Campaign*, 79.

34. Margolick, *Promise and the Dream*, 292.

35. Clarke, *Last Campaign*, 79.

36. Clarke, *Last Campaign*, 153.

37. Clarke, *Last Campaign*, 158.

38. Clarke, *Last Campaign*, 159.

39. Clarke, *Last Campaign*, 159.

40. Clarke, *Last Campaign*, 160.

41. Steven W. Bender, *One Night in America: Robert Kennedy, César Chávez, and the Dream of Dignity* (Boulder: Paradigm, 2008), 8.

42. Bender, *One Night in America*, 27.

43. Bender, *One Night in America*, 34.

44. Sidorenko, *Robert F. Kennedy*, 160–61.

45. Clarke, *Last Campaign*, 252.

46. Sidorenko, *Robert F. Kennedy*, 161.

47. Jules Witcover, *85 Days: The Last Campaign of Robert Kennedy* (New York: William Morrow, 1988), 199.

48. Dyson, *What Truth Sounds Like*, 16–17, 264.

49. Ali Michael, "Rachel Dolezal Syndrome," Educating for Equity (blog), https://tinyurl.com/ps5llrv.

50. Timothy J. Lensmire, *White Folks: Race and Identity in Rural America* (New York: Routledge, 2017), 7, 45.

51. James Baldwin, *The Fire Next Time* (New York: Vintage International, 1993), 21–22.

52. Matthew W. Hughey, "Hegemonic Whiteness: From Structure and

Agency to Identity Allegiance," in *The Construction of Whiteness: An Interdisciplinary Analysis of Race Formation and the Meaning of a White Identity*, ed. Stephen Middleton, David R. Roediger, and Donald M. Shaffer (Jackson: University Press of Mississippi, 2016), 230.

53. Hughey, "Hegemonic Whiteness," 230.

54. Hughey, "Hegemonic Whiteness," 231.

55. Becky Thompson and Veronica T. Watson, "Theorizing White Racial Trauma and Its Remedies," in Middleton et al., *Construction of Whiteness*, 234.

56. Thompson and Watson, "Theorizing White Racial Trauma and Its Remedies," 235.

57. Thompson and Watson, "Theorizing White Racial Trauma and Its Remedies," 236.

58. Robin DiAngelo, *What Does It Mean to Be White? Developing White Racial Literacy*, rev. ed. (New York: Peter Lang, 2016), 247.

59. DiAngelo, "What Does It Mean to Be White?," 248.

60. DiAngelo, "What Does It Mean to Be White?," 250.

61. Thompson and Watson, "Theorizing White Racial Trauma and Its Remedies," 247.

62. Thompson and Watson, "Theorizing White Racial Trauma and Its Remedies," 241, 242.

63. Wilson Harris, "Creoleness: The Crossroads of a Civilization?," in *Caribbean Creolization: Reflections on the Cultural Dynamics of Language, Literature, and Identity*, ed. Kathleen M. Balutansky and Marie-Agnès Sourieau (Gainesville: University Press of Florida, 1998), 26.

64. Thompson and Watson, "Theorizing White Racial Trauma and Its Remedies," 248.

65. W. E. B. Du Bois coined this term in *The Souls of Black Folk* (Chicago: A. C. McClurg, 1903).

66. Thompson and Watson, "Theorizing White Racial Trauma and Its Remedies," 249.

67. Bohrer, *Revolution of Robert Kennedy*, 8.

68. Thompson and Watson, "Theorizing White Racial Trauma and Its Remedies," 250.

6

Harlem and Howard: Creolization of Curtiss Paul DeYoung

CURTISS PAUL DEYOUNG

"I don't know the rhyme or reason—why he continues to put himself, not in the same situation but in similar [ones], that are outside his comfort zone. He thrives on stretching himself, on pushing the envelope." These words were spoken by my wife, Karen DeYoung, and quoted in an article by journalist Frank Clancy, who profiled my role in developing a new reconciliation studies degree program at Bethel University in St. Paul, Minnesota. In that same article, Clancy converses with my long-term mentor, the late Dr. James Earl Massey. Clancy wrote that Massey described what he called my "'internalized openness,' a way of looking at others without judgment that is, like the habit of saying 'thank you,' so deeply ingrained in his being that it's become 'a life trait' . . . 'the way his own heart told him to go: openness to all.'" Massey continued: "It is my belief that a person who grows up in America is subjected to many forces which deter their openness to other persons. When you find someone who has a kind of natural openness and raises questions about what's going on in our society—'Why *can't* we be together? Why *can't* we live as one?'—that shows me the divine that is necessary in order to be a leader."[1]

My life journey did not begin in a place of internalized openness.[2] I was born and raised in whiteness. While not Amish, I was born in the very white rural communities of northwest Indiana known as "Amish country." My ancestors were mostly Dutch and English—the nations of colonizers and slave traders. My school years were spent in white suburbia. My high school graduating class was over 99 percent white. I enrolled in a predominately white middle-class Christian college located in a region where the Ku Klux Klan was still active. After college I moved to a small town with a population of five thousand mostly white people. My identity was shaped by the ways that society constructs or defines my reality—white, male, Christian, Protestant, middle-class, educated, able-bodied, heterosexual, English speaking, and a citizen of the United States of America—a nice, white, Anglo-Saxon Protestant (WASP). I was on track to live a comfortable, one-dimensional life that was in line with my WASP middle-class status.

While mostly white, my upbringing was not exclusively white. During my preschool years in the early 1960s, my father was the pastor of a racially diverse congregation in Dowagiac, Michigan. I do not have memories of this, and I am not certain whether it had any direct effect on me. But it changed the way my parents thought about race issues in the United States. When I was twelve, my father and I watched the documentary *King: A Filmed Record . . . Montgomery to Memphis*. This caused me to explore further Martin Luther King Jr.'s life and learn more about racism in the United States. I read every book on King I could find and listened to recordings of his sermons. At Anderson College (now Anderson University), I met Dr. James Earl Massey, the college's dean of chapel and professor of biblical studies. He was one of the very few, if not the only, African American campus pastors at a predominately white Christian institution of higher learning in the 1960s to 1970s. Dr. Massey was mentored by African American mystic theologian Howard Thurman and close friends with Martin Luther King Jr. He opened a world of ideas about racial justice and reconciliation. These moments were whispers of a reality I knew through books and documentaries. The first twenty-three years of my existence were rooted in whiteness.

IMMERSION INTO OTHERNESS AND OPPRESSION

After serving for one year after college as small-town youth pastor in Michigan, I moved to New York City to work with youth at a Times Square homeless shelter. This was the early 1980s when Times Square was the center of the sex industry in the United States and a magnet for people who were homeless. The move to New York City was a dramatic change for me. I left a monocultural, monolingual small town for the largest city in the United States, which was home to people from a multiplicity of cultures, races, and languages. In New York, I lived as a part of the Covenant House faith community, a Franciscan-styled Roman Catholic lay community. I was a Protestant attending daily Mass and participating in a prayer life that included chanting of the Psalms. New York City, Times Square, Catholic Mass, and the like were places where I felt way outside of my comfort zone.

One Sunday morning I decided to find some comfort in a church of my own denomination. I entered the subway station and rode the A train to 145th Street. There I transferred to the AA local and rode to the stop at 155th Street. I walked a few blocks to my destination and opened the front door of the Congregational Church of God. I was unaware that 154th Street and Amsterdam Avenue is in the northern section of Harlem, a cultural mecca for African Americans. An usher greeted me by asking, "May I help you?" A white person had not walked through those doors in many years. I replied that I was a member of the Church of God and a recent graduate from Anderson College, a Church of God–affiliated school in Anderson, Indiana. I was then ushered into the sanctuary and seated in the front next to some seasoned members of the congregation. The worship service had begun, although the pastor was nowhere in sight. (I would later learn that this was called the devotional service and led by lay members.)

A few minutes later I was directed to the office of Pastor Levorn Aaron. Dr. Aaron noted that he had been informed of my presence and that I was a member of the Church of God and a graduate of Anderson College. He asked if I knew his friend Dr. James Earl Massey—the esteemed biblical scholar and preacher in residence at Anderson College and School of Theology. I assured Pastor Aaron that I indeed did know his friend Dr. Massey and had taken several courses from him. Pastor Aaron next asked if I was a minister. I responded that I was not yet ordained but had been licensed as a minister. He then opened his calendar of church activities and asked if I could preach at the congregation on the Sunday morning two weeks following. I had only been in the church building for a matter of minutes, and now I was being asked to preach. I said yes. Thus began, as journalist Clancy wrote, "the experience that would truly shape DeYoung's life."[3] I preached on Sunday mornings nearly once a month during the year I lived in New York City. Rev. Aaron and the congregation taught me how to preach. I learned to slow my pace and treat preaching as a dialogue rather than a monologue. The congregation encouraged and supported me with their verbal responses. Dr. Aaron designated me his associate minister—"Minister Curt"—and trained me in urban ministry as his apprentice. For one year, on Sundays and Wednesday evenings, I was immersed in the black experience at Congregational Church of God in the African American cultural mecca of Harlem, New York.

Nearly twenty years later in December 2000, I returned to New York City to participate in the funeral of Dr. Levorn Aaron. He was eighty years old when he died. I had visited Rev. Aaron and the Congregational Church of God on numerous occasions since leaving New York in 1982. I had an open invitation to preach whenever I was in the area. I accepted that invitation many times. The church was full the day of the funeral. I was introduced as a son of the Congregational Church of God. The casket, which had been closed during the service, was opened again for everyone to have a final viewing of the body. When the ministers were called to walk by the casket, I stopped to speak to Mrs. Aaron and their five daughters. I did not recall ever having met any of Reverend Aaron's daughters. Yet each of them hugged me and greeted me as "Curt" (which was what Pastor Aaron called me). Each of them said, in almost the same words, "Curt, our dad loved you so much!" Then they would mention how much he talked about me and how they had seen all our family photos sent to the Aarons each Christmas. I felt like I was experiencing a homecoming.

John Blake of CNN.com interviewed me for his article, "When You Are the Only White Person in the Room." He asked how the immersion into the Harlem church community had affected me. He recounts my response:

> One day, DeYoung was looking through a journal he started keeping after he joined the church in Harlem. He noticed that the word "black" rang through every passage: I'm going to this "black church," I'm eating "black food," I'm making "black friends." He recalled that no one at the Harlem church had ever placed a racial modifier before his name. "Never once in that entire year did they refer to me as being white," he says. "I was just a member of the congregation. I was a child of God." DeYoung kept reading and scanned the journal entries that came after he spent more time in the church. He noticed he was still writing about making new friends, listening to gospel and eating good food. The word "black," however, had disappeared from his journal. They were no longer "the other." He was no longer an outsider. He was at home.[4]

A year after leaving New York City, I moved to Washington, DC, for what would be a nearly three-year immersion into the black community at another African American mecca. Ta-Nehisi Coates writes in his book *Between the World and Me*, "My only Mecca was, is, and shall be Howard University. . . . The history, the location, the alumni combined to create The Mecca—the crossroads of the black diaspora."[5] I arrived in Washington, DC, for a two-month internship at Third Street Church of God. I planned at the end of the summer to return to New York, where

I was enrolled at Union Theological Seminary and Columbia University. The congregation was evenly divided between African Americans and Jamaicans. I met the woman who is now my wife on my very first Sunday there. So I inquired of the church's pastoral staff where I might attend seminary in DC while I considered this newly developing relationship. As black pastors in DC, they recommended Howard University School of Divinity.

Being educated at a Historically Black College and University (HBCU) added a needed critical analysis to the experiential portion of my immersion process. This led to a deeper dive than my one year at a church in Harlem. It was full immersion: education at an HBCU, membership at a black church, life in a majority African American city, and close relationships with my wife's African American family. Howard University School of Divinity taught me about racism, the black church, liberation theology, Afrocentric biblical interpretation, and life in African American contexts. The three years at Howard University were advanced training in antiracism and critical cultural competency fully integrated into my education and daily life. My ways of thinking and analysis were all challenged; some parts were discarded and replaced, and all were transformed. After graduation, I wrote Dean Lawrence Jones of the School of Divinity and thanked him for the Howard University education and how it taught me to think critically. I felt like I had gone through a brain transplant. I arrived thinking one way but left completely changed. For example, after taking several courses at Howard University School of Divinity, I had become conversant in black liberation theology. I had a conversation with Dr. Samuel Hines, my pastor at Third Street Church of God in Washington, DC, and originally from Jamaica. At the time, he was not convinced about black theology. As a white man raised in white suburbs, I was arguing for black theology while my black pastor was arguing against it. The words I was saying were those of my Howard University professors. The language did not match my background or my look. It represented my growing competency in the ways of thinking and expressing myself in my new social location.

I also gained a set of mentors at Howard University.[6] Among them was Dr. Calvin Morris. He had worked with both Martin Luther King Jr. and Jesse Jackson Sr. Morris has a razor-sharp ability to cut to the real issues when dealing with individuals who aspire to leadership. He cared deeply about his students at Howard University. This concern often translated into a confrontational style that pressed all of a student's emotional buttons in a very forceful manner. Morris would remark, "If you cannot take a little pressure at the seminary, you will never survive in a local congregation." He applied some of that pressure to me in the classroom, his office, and in the hallways. Morris knew and respected my mentor Dr. Massey. But he considered Massey's style to be more diplomatic. Morris believed I needed to learn how to deal with a strong, angry black man without racializing the experience. He also knew I needed to address some deep issues before I could move forward in the process of working for racial justice.

Dr. Morris performed surgery on my psyche and touched a nerve. I found myself growing angry at his constant confrontation. Not only was I upset by his behavior, my frustration became hatred—an emotion I had not experienced before. I needed to repent of my hate and confess directly to Dr. Morris. I arranged to meet with him at his office. After exposing my soul, he replied that he had been waiting for me to come to him. I perceived his response as arrogant and became even angrier. Morris was pushing me because he knew I needed to mature. Over time I began to understand that he had my best interest in mind. Calvin Morris was essential to my full immersion at The Mecca, Howard University.

I have discovered that immersion into the realities of oppression and the building of transformational relationships must become a way of life for whites. The seduction of whiteness and privilege is powerful. Whites can always return to a life of privilege. Therefore, I have intentionally found ways to remain immersed in the African American community. After Harlem and Howard, I sought out and maintained such transformational relationships. I regularly placed myself in black-dominant spaces for continued formation, learning, and mentorship.[7] I have gone to great lengths in listening to and learning from persons of many races and cultures. This education occurred to a lesser degree at Wounded Knee on the Pine Ridge Indian Reservation, in the Hmong communities of St. Paul and Minneapolis, and in various Latinx settings. I have invited women to speak truth into my life. I have submitted to the authority of persons of color and women at work, church, and in life. I have read widely and discussed endlessly the perspectives informed by worldviews shaped in cultures and settings unlike my own. When I was a professor, I invited students of color, Native Americans, women, LGBTQ persons, students with disabilities, and others who were marginalized in various ways to share deeply with me of their journeys.

My early formative years as a young adult in Harlem and at Howard shaped within me a way to relax into cultural settings not my own. I eventually was often able to seamlessly shift my frame of reference and modify my behavior to adapt culturally. This same notion, perspective, and way of relaxing into other cultural contexts travels with me to South Africa, where I have experienced immersion and developed deep relationships in black African, mixed-race Coloured, and Indian contexts.[8] It travels with me to Palestine and Israel with a growing ease of cultural embrace in multiple contexts.[9] It made my experience in Guadeloupean Creole culture possible—even though I could not speak Creole or French. My language translators also became my cultural interpreters and educators. Finding invitation and entrance via these experts in their own culture enabled me to listen, experience, and learn in authentic ways. A similar approach travels with me into interreligious and interfaith spaces. It began as I relaxed into Catholicism in the Covenant Faith Community in New York and later as I studied with aspiring Dominican priests in DC. (For a Protestant, being immersed in Catholic settings felt like an interreligious move until I discovered the many Christian commonalities.) It travels with me into Muslim and Jewish spaces in the Holy Land and elsewhere.

I experienced a re-immersion into communities facing racial injustice and learned new and recently emerging realities when I moved to Chicago in 2014. Having lived so many years in Minneapolis, I was given access to diverse spaces there because I was known and had deep relationships. Upon arrival in Chicago, I discovered I had grown soft in Minneapolis. In Chicago I was not known. I was a white man from the white state of Minnesota. No one cared what my experiences might have been or what books I might have authored. I had to once again earn my right to be present in diverse black and Latinx spaces. I was also reminded that Chicago's communities of color differ in certain ways from Minneapolis and St. Paul. I arrived in Chicago during the emergence of Black Lives Matter. I was held suspect in millennial black spaces. I had no credibility in most Chicago spaces and was considered a white outsider with questionable intentions. But I stayed in confrontive and uncomfortable black spaces, listening and learning even though I often felt unwelcome. I also sought out some of the young black leaders for one-on-ones to accelerate my re-entry and re-education.[10] I have discovered and decided that immersion, challenge, confrontation, listening, learning—the awful grace of God—are all required and nonnegotiable parts of an ongoing, lifelong creolization process for whites and privileged people.

DISCOVERING A HEALED WHITE IDENTITY

I have been introduced in African American settings as white on the outside but black on the inside. I remarked when leaving an organization that was trying to increase its percentage of persons of color on staff that my departure would bring the organization closer to this goal. An African American coworker informed me that I did not count as white. I was called a white soul brother by a Jamaican colleague, and a black South African wrote to me, "I say to you may the good God bless you, stay as a black man in a white skin." Afrocentric biblical scholar and my former professor and mentor from Howard University Dr. Cain Hope Felder wrote in the foreword of my first book,

> Here are the fruits and scholarship of a European-American minister and social activist who has uniquely chosen to sit where many so-called minorities have had to sit. He thereby writes as one who knows what it is to be an alien in your native land and to some extent marginalized because of choosing to break from the pack and to look at the social chaos and injustice of those below who hurt.[11]

Of course, this is all very affirming. Yet I am still a white male! While I may have acquired an intellectual stance usually reserved for persons of color and even acculturated some patterns from other cultures, I will never experience life as a person of color. As a white male in the United States, I benefit from a history and present reality that have given me significant advantages and privileges. I am protected from the many daily indignities, microaggressions, and reduction in life choices experienced by others because of racism, sexism, and injustice.

Ten years ago, when I was fifty, I wrote a memoir, *Homecoming: A "White" Man's Journey from Harlem to Jerusalem*. In my reflections I asked the following questions about my identity:

> As a white male with birthright advantage and privilege . . . am I trapped forever in "whiteness" and "maleness"? Is this definition of my identity cast in concrete? Or can I find my true, God-created humanity and experience a primal homecoming? Is it possible to embrace a new "view" of myself as a "multicultural" person—not limited by a history of racism created by the system within which I live?[12]

My reality is I have been raised white with all the benefits and privileges that pertain to whiteness in the United States. What I need is a healed white identity as described in chapter 5. One where I refuse to wear the garments of whiteness and privilege. My creolized identity journey is a process toward greater self-knowledge that creates dissonance and disruption. This crisis of identity occurs because the new self-awareness comes from an ongoing examination of injustice in society through a firsthand glimpse of the life narratives of those directly affected by oppression. I feel like I live in the place of identity chaos where perspectives collide and viewpoints crash. My white, middle-class origins whisper an inviting appeal to return to a life of privilege far from cries of pain and suffering. My journeys into oppression and injustice call me to solidarity and outrage. The creolization process creates chaos for whites. We exist in the tension between privilege and oppression. We face an ongoing process of interrogating and reconfiguring whiteness. We discover the possibilities for a healed white identity as we welcome creolization.

HEALING AND HUMANIZING

I was welcomed as a child of God by members of a church in Harlem. They embraced me as a person, a human being. My identity was not reduced to social identifiers. I was not treated differently because of my whiteness. This community of faith reflected back to me total acceptance. I glimpsed my essence as a human being. What a healing moment! Yet throughout my life I have had to face my own revelations of racism. John Blake described my first realization that I had been marked by whiteness.

> When DeYoung was in college, he decided he was going to introduce himself to an attractive white freshman he spotted. But when he saw the woman walking across campus with two black men, he suddenly lost interest. DeYoung rummaged through his mental attic to figure out why. The answer humbled him. He was a man who grew up buying the Rev. Martin Luther King's speeches and watching his father pastor a multiracial church, but he unearthed something ugly. "I had fallen prey to the stereotype that a white woman involved with a black man is damaged goods, which goes back to the slave masters who taught people that black men were sexual animals," he says. "I thought, 'I don't have prejudice,' and then one of the oldest stereotypes struck me right in the face."[13]

The experience at the church in Harlem helped me reduce the racist stereotypes I had held and limit the occurrences like that in college. But there were deeper matters that had not yet surfaced. Ten years after leaving New York City, a Minneapolis coworker asked me to purchase a hat called a kufi for him on a trip back to New York City. He said that such a hat could be found at a marketplace near the Apollo Theater in the heart of Harlem. I had been in Harlem on a regular basis during my tenure at the Congregational Church of God. While I had never been to this particular section of Harlem before, I had always been at ease as a white person in the African American cultural mecca. It was a sunny summer day in the marketplace. Vendors were selling items that exhibited the colors of Africa and shirts that displayed Malcolm X's face. As soon as I stepped onto the streets of Harlem, I was gripped by an intense and emotionally raw fear. I felt intimidated as the only white person surrounded by hundreds of black people. All the negative social images I had inherited or acquired about African Americans flashed across my mind. I tried to reassert control of my thoughts and emotions. I reminded myself that I had no reason to fear. The marketplace was safe, and people were shopping or attending to their daily activities. My imagination had been taken captive by deeply ingrained stereotypes. I told myself that the people in Harlem that day were not plotting revenge against me because of my white skin. Yet I could not free myself from these debilitating feelings of anxiety and fear. I was clearly having a whiteness panic attack.

Unable to restore my equilibrium, or find the hat, I left Harlem. Then my emotions calmed. As I rode the subway back to the lower part of Manhattan and away from Harlem, I was troubled that my life experience, analysis of racism, and belief in reconciliation could not prevent my intense reaction. I was embarrassed. How could I experience such feelings? I had been married to an African American woman for several years, and we had children who were defined as black. I certainly did not believe any of the stereotypes that paraded through my mind on this visit to Harlem. Finally, I realized that I needed healing from inherited beliefs, irrational fears, and guilty feelings that resulted from being raised in a society where white dominance had harmed generations of people of color. Sociologist Becky Thompson and literary critic Veronica T. Watson call this "the trauma of whiteness."[14] As a white person in the United States, I also am wounded by racism, albeit often unknowingly. Many whites are not aware of the invisible scars we carry on our souls due to racism and the unearned privilege of a white supremacist system.[15]

REVOLUTIONIZING SOCIETY

In preparation for graduation from the School of Divinity at Howard University, I had a farewell conversation with Dr. Calvin Morris. The essence of his advice to me was, "You have enjoyed Howard. I am sure you want to stay with us [blacks]. But you need to take what you have

learned here and go back to white communities to address the source
of racism. Continue to build community with us but go to whites. We
have prepared you to work for change in white communities." Morris
was challenging me to disrupt the racial status quo in white communities. It was a prophetic and revolutionary word. As I have reflected on
my life journey, Dr. Morris's words have been a consistent theme—dare
I say, God's calling. My journey post-Howard took me from black DC
to white Minnesota. I led a Minneapolis church to move from being
white-dominant to the beginning of becoming multiracial. I led a faith-
based nonprofit organization in Minneapolis–St. Paul with token representation from communities of color to elect a board of directors that
was majority people of color, hire a staff that matched the cities' demographics, and make racial justice and reconciliation central to its work.
I established an academic degree program in reconciliation studies at a
university that was 90 percent white. The program focus sought to disrupt the racism of white students in order to build skills to challenge
racism in their white communities and to empower students of color to
survive toxic white spaces in order to find their own voices. Through
the years, I have also written books and articles addressing racism that
are read in white communities. I followed Dr. Morris's prophetic and
revolutionary words with some success, always challenging structures of
whiteness.

I was invited in 2014 to be the executive director of Community
Renewal Society (CRS), a historic racial justice organization in Chicago.
CRS had partnered with Martin Luther King Jr.'s Southern Christian
Leadership Conference (SCLC) as part of the Chicago Freedom Move-
ment in 1966. King associate James Bevel had joined the staff of CRS to
prepare for King's arrival in Chicago, and he had merged the staffs of
SCLC with CRS on the West Side of Chicago.[16] The engagement with
SCLC and the Civil Rights Movement transformed and reframed CRS.
By the 1990s Dr. Yvonne Delk became the first African American executive director of CRS. She was succeeded by my former Howard University professor Calvin Morris, who led Community Renewal Society
in the first decade of the twenty-first century. I accepted the job at CRS
with this history in mind, assuming that it was a fully multiracial organization. My son Jonathan reminded me of the prophetic and revolutionary words of Dr. Morris. He asked if it was appropriate for me to move
away from white-dominant organizations. Somewhat dismissively, I told
him I had paid my dues with nearly thirty years of challenging white
institutions.

What I discovered was that Community Renewal Society was a

majority-white organization with a stated mission of racial justice in a city where whites were only one-third of the population when I arrived in 2014. Following the retirement of Calvin Morris, and after twenty-five years of black leadership at the executive level, CRS drifted white. I was the new white male executive director arriving in Chicago from Minneapolis with limited knowledge of the history of Community Renewal Society. I had assumed that as a racial justice organization with such a history, CRS would reflect the demographic realities of the city of Chicago. Given my education at an HBCU seminary, I knew that this internal, white-dominant racial reality at CRS and my hiring as a white male executive director posed serious questions of integrity. Black leadership at the executive director level (as was the case with Delk and Morris) clearly was not enough to fully transform the organization. I discovered that the board of directors had always been majority white. While a black executive director or black board chair may signify that an organization is "black led," as along as whites control the board of directors, the organization is owned by whiteness.

Unexpectedly, Calvin Morris's prophetic calling still defined my work, even at Community Renewal Society. So I asked some white board members to leave the board and make room for persons of color at the table. Within a year and a half, the board became majority black. The board that was 52 percent white when I arrived was only 27 percent white when I left in 2017. CRS became a "black owned" organization, with a majority of the board African American. This transformation completely changed the conversation at the "ownership" level. With a black-led board of directors, the demographic transformation of the staff followed. When I left CRS in 2017, the board and staff were majority black. Letting go of the levers of power is not easy for whites, even when their intentions are positive social change. For CRS to become black-led, the white executive director had to leave. After three years, I resigned to make room for full transformation.[17] Creolization calls for and creates revolution. Sometimes the impact of revolutionary action has a personal price.

Calvin Morris said I had been educated at Howard University to go into white spaces to challenge white supremacy and racial injustice. Such action is revolutionary. My life-long creolization process has meant ongoing immersion in communities of color, so I can be healed, re-formed, and transformed for the purpose of returning to and disrupting white dominant spaces, thereby opening the door for people of color to enter and redeem white spaces—to transform them into Creole-like communities. Therein lies hope.

Notes

1. Frank Clancy, "The Reconciler," *Minnesota Monthly*, June 2004, 60.

2. Many of the stories in this chapter have appeared elsewhere, including Curtiss Paul DeYoung, *Homecoming: A "White" Man's Journey through Harlem to Jerusalem* (Eugene, OR: Wipf & Stock, 2015); Drick Boyd, *White Allies in the Struggle for Racial Justice* (Maryknoll, NY: Orbis, 2015), 253–69; John Blake, "When You Are the Only White Person in the Room," CNN.com, September 11, 2014, https://tinyurl.com/yc2pncqn; Clancy, "Reconciler," 56–61; Michael O. Emerson and Christian Smith, *Divided by Faith: Evangelical Religion and the Problem of Race in America* (New York: Oxford University Press, 2000), 60–62.

3. Clancy, "Reconciler," 58.

4. Blake, "When You Are the Only White Person in the Room."

5. Ta-Nehisi Coates, *Between the World and Me* (New York: Spiegl & Grau, 2015), 39–40.

6. See DeYoung, *Homecoming*, 32–35.

7. Some examples are strong black clergy relationships in Minneapolis and St. Paul and regular engagement with the Samuel DeWitt Proctor Conference. I sought out Rev. Jeremiah Wright for regular mentoring during the years I lived in Chicago.

8. I have been to South Africa on fourteen occasions. See DeYoung, *Homecoming*, 99–111.

9. I have been to the Holy Land on five occasions. For description of first two visits see DeYoung, *Homecoming*, 113–27.

10. One of the young activists I met with periodically was Charlene Carruthers of the Black Youth Project 100 (BYP100). Her book *Unapologetic: A Black, Queer, and Feminist Mandate for Radical Movements* (Boston: Beacon, 2018) is a good representation of the mentoring I received from young black activists I encountered in Chicago.

11. Cain Hope Felder, foreword to Curtiss Paul DeYoung, *Coming Together: The Bible's Message in an Age of Diversity* (Valley Forge, PA: Judson, 1995), x.

12. DeYoung, *Homecoming*, 55.

13. Blake, "When You Are the Only White Person in the Room." See also Clancy, "Reconciler," 60; and Curtiss Paul DeYoung, *Reconciliation: Our Greatest Challenge, Our Only Hope* (Valley Forge, PA: Judson, 1997), 63.

14. Becky Thompson and Veronica T. Watson, "Theorizing White Racial Trauma and Its Remedies," in *The Construction of Whiteness: An Interdisci-*

plinary Analysis of Race Formation and the Meaning of a White Identity, ed. Stephen Middleton, David R. Roediger, and Donald M. Shaffer (Jackson: University Press of Mississippi, 2016), 234.

15.   See DeYoung, *Homecoming*, 46–48; and DeYoung, *Reconciliation*, 118–19.

16.   James R. Ralph Jr., *Northern Protest: Martin Luther King, Jr., Chicago, and the Civil Rights Movement* (Cambridge: Harvard University Press, 1993), 44. See also Mary Lou Finley et al., eds., *The Chicago Freedom Movement: Martin Luther King Jr. and Civil Rights Activism in the North* (Lexington: University Press of Kentucky, 2016).

17.   For a fuller history of race and my time at Community Renewal Society, see Curtiss Paul DeYoung, "Racial Equity and Faith-Based Organizing at Community Renewal Society," in *Urban Ministry Reconsidered: Contexts and Approaches*, ed. R. Drew Smith, Stephanie C. Boddie, and Ronald E. Peters (Louisville: Westminster John Knox, 2018), 89–96.

7.

Cave of Machpelah: Creolization at Religious Intersections

CURTISS PAUL DEYOUNG

When the patriarch Abraham died at age 175 years, "His sons Isaac and Ishmael buried him in the cave of Machpelah, in the field of Ephron son of Zohar the Hittite, east of Mamre, the field that Abraham purchased from the Hittites. There Abraham was buried, with his wife Sarah" (Gen 25:9–10).[1] The scriptural stories of Ishmael and Isaac portray broken family relationships and reveal much dissension in the broader human family. God intended that both Ishmael and Isaac would be the progenitors of nations. The death of Abraham provided an opportunity for his sons—and the nations they produced—to move beyond problematic histories and convoluted relationships into a future of restored human family. The death of the patriarch was a rare moment when the past could be put aside. Divided nations and tribes could reconnect. Reconciled relationships offered fresh possibilities. It seems that Ishmael and Isaac left the cave without reconciliation. But the possibility of reconciliation as they buried their father in the cave is a compelling image.

We stand at the symbolic cave of Machpelah today, peering in to see the death of patriarchy and racial hierarchy. While these deaths are not yet final, a history dominated by white males is slowly passing away. Women and persons of color are liberating history and writing a new future. This book hopes to spur the development of the mindsets and skills necessary for leadership and community in this hoped-for future. The Creole metaphor; the ideas of adaptation, critical cultural competency, and critical white double consciousness; and the awful grace of God have opened conceptional windows alongside Scripture and present-day narratives. While not explicitly discussed in this book, the

Creole-like reality of the collaborative nomenclature LGBTQI and the growing awareness of gender fluidity will also contribute to the reshaping of culture in the years ahead.

This book is written from a faith perspective. Yet often, people of faith and religious communities are resistant to the perspectives and skills proposed here. Religion itself has at times been an oppressive and divisive force. Still, religious texts call for unity and social justice. The adherents of religious faiths need to develop skills for liberation and reconciliation. What could a creolization of religion look like? The burial of Abraham frames an interfaith encounter at the very origins of the Abrahamic faiths. In the story of human religion, Ishmael is a spiritual ancestor of Islam, and his younger brother Isaac serves as a spiritual ancestor for both Judaism and Christianity. The story in Genesis 25 of Ishmael and Isaac coming together in Hebron to bury their father Abraham provides a compelling image and a biblical call for the creolization of religious difference.[2] The cave of Machpelah is a metaphor for interfaith competency that calls us today to build relational bridges across a wide range of religious differences in the twenty-first century. Peace and religion scholar Rabbi Marc Gopin notes that what we have is "a rare example of what I would call intermythic conversation. Jews and Muslims [and Christians] share the mythic origins of their respective communities in Isaac and Ishmael and wisely highlight an overarching family unity."[3] This final chapter moves the conversation of Creoleness into the realm of religion, an important discussion for a multi-faith world.

DEVELOPMENTAL MODEL FOR INTERRELIGIOUS SENSITIVITY

Rabbi Marc Gopin's fellow peace and religion scholar Dr. Mohammed Abu-Nimer was the first person to develop an interreligious complement to sociologist Milton Bennett's Developmental Model for Intercultural Sensitivity (DMIS) to conceptualize interreligious competence.[4] He replaces "intercultural" with "interreligious." As noted in earlier chapters, adaptation is the stage in the DMIS where one has the ability to cognitively frame shift and behaviorally code switch from one's own culture of origin to another. In this case one would shift from their religious frame of reference of origin to another. Abu-Nimer writes, "The adaptation stage described by Bennett does not involve assimilation into another culture, but rather temporarily and intentionally shifting one's cultural frame of reference (empathy) or adopting multiple permanent frames of reference (pluralism)"[5]—in other words, "the ability to alter perception and behavior to appropriately suit different religious contexts."[6]

From 1996 to 1999, Abu-Nimer engaged with participants from differing religious backgrounds in interviews and workshops on interreligious peacemaking to gain their perspective on his religious-adapted DMIS. He notes,

> Very few participants were able to imagine adapting this way in their religious lives. Most felt they could not shift into a different religious system even temporarily without threatening their own religious identity or credibility in their community. . . . Many participants agreed that it is easier to achieve empathy in an intercultural setting than in an interreligious setting because it does not so strongly challenge their moral values, ethics, or faith. This inability to temporarily adopt another's religion or faith might be difficult to overcome because of the intensity of empathy in a faith setting.[7]

Abu-Nimer suggested two possible conclusions from his findings: "The intercultural developmental model was not fully transferable in an interreligious setting and integrating religious perspectives was undesirable. [Or] another interpretation is that religious identity is more central (perhaps meaningful) for individuals than other aspects of cultural identity."[8] It seems that for people of faith, their religious faith has a stronger claim on their sense of identity than their culture.

Professor of conflict studies Hizkias Assefa shares a story that prompts further consideration of Abu-Nimer's discussion on religious adaptation. Assefa describes an experience in which "both Christian and Muslim participants were able to go beyond their religious identities and meet at a spiritual meeting point where they could look critically at their behavior with, as the participants put it, 'God as a witness.'" He explains,

> If the process manages to get the parties to that point, there is a powerful meeting place there, which can unleash tremendous possibilities for honesty and reconciliation. Although this author was raised a Christian and practices that faith, in one of these workshops a Muslim Sheik commented to me: "You may not know it, but you are deeply Muslim." That was indication that we were drinking from the same spiritual fountain, although we came at it from different religious entry points.[9]

Mohammed Abu-Nimer describes the process of adaptation as beginning with empathy.[10] He writes,

> Religious empathy occurs when the believer is actually ready to experience (temporarily, for an hour, a day, or a month) another spiritual path and to be able to understand (for a brief period) the other's religious meaning, con-

text, and points of reference. An example of such a situational reaction is when a Muslim agrees to participate in a prayer with Christians or Jews in their houses of prayer and to be willing to spiritually connect and experience Christians' or Jews' unique ways of connecting to God.[11]

A noted example from two 1960s anti–Vietnam War activists illustrates this experience. Father Daniel Berrigan, a Christian, shared the Eucharist with Zen Master Thich Nhat Hanh, a Vietnamese Buddhist, who recited a reading from the Heart Sutra. They temporarily shifted into the other's religious ceremonial experience.[12] Abu–Nimer describes the process: "Rituals create a mode of dialogue. Understanding another religion's rituals opens a window into the meaning of the other. Participating in another's rituals allows [one] to temporarily experience the other's worldview."[13] Developing empathy through engaging in religious rituals helps one develop greater interreligious competency.

Abu–Nimer contends that over time one can develop a more advanced form of adaptation "in which one person has developed two [or more] religious frames of reference." He explains,

> Spirituality can be experienced and lived through two religious paths. The person can operate in both religions and understand, accept, and internalize the religious meanings and codes in both of them [and] has developed a consciousness that not only integrates the two religions, but also is able to criticize and pass judgment on both. . . . Such change in religious identity only occurs over many years of spiritual exploration and discoveries and of intrareligious and interreligious experiences.[14]

At religious adaptation one can shift religiously back and forth in the same way a bilingual person interchanges language when speaking.

Psychologist Steven J. Sandage and Boston University doctoral student Jonathan Morgan used Abu–Nimer's conclusions as a foundation for their own study of interreligious competency.[15] They consider Catholic monk Thomas Merton's interaction with Buddhist D. T. Suzuki. Merton wrote, "There is the possibility of contact on a deep level between this contemplative and monastic tradition in the West and the various contemplative traditions of the East."[16] Morgan and Sandage express that Merton was not looking for a universal or assimilated religion. They note, "Within his actions he is able to integrate insights and practices from Zen Buddhism, as shared with him by DT Suzuki, with his own Cistercian contemplative practices. This demonstrates great flexibility of spiritual identity, able to encounter a similar ground through different religious symbols-systems."[17] Morgan and Sandage also point to mystic theologian Howard Thurman's exploration of "common ground," where "he suggests the possibility of contact that occurs through the hard work of self-knowledge and security, alongside a deep commitment to something, like social justice, that extends beyond the individual."[18]

What Sandage and Morgan describe is similar to how religious mystics speak of their experience. Mystics often do not recognize religious boundaries. As Sufi scholar Seyyed Hossein Nasr writes, "Every authentic spirituality has its distinct perfume which is an extension of the perfume of paradise and reflects the celestial archetype that is the primal reality of the spirituality in question."[19] Mystics experience the divine presence within a realm that is spiritual and not institutional. Howard Thurman wrote, "The goal of the mystic, therefore, is to know God in a comprehensive sense; for God is grasped by the whole self or the whole self is laid hold upon by God—the vision of God is realized inclusively."[20] Mystics seek to know God as God—not through the narrow interpretive lens of a particular religious or faith expression. While deeply rooted in their own faith tradition, contemplatives rarely feel bound by a religious tradition when seeking union with the Divine. Embracing a mystic mindset allows for the development of interreligious competence.

Mohammed Abu-Nimer found that participants in his workshops often rejected religious adaptation.[21] Adaptation was believed to lead to religious conversion and "the loss of one's perceived authentic religious identity." Interreligious competence was "dismissed as inauthentic and viewed as a phenomenon that can endanger the very existence of any interfaith group."[22] Abu-Nimer and coauthors Amal I. Khoury and Emily Welty address the concern of losing one's own religious faith in the exploration of other religious frames of reference. They write, "It is important to note that the development of intercultural competence and improved cross-religious group relations is not based on the 'surrender' of one's own cultural or religious identity or practices. Rather, the development of such competence is focused on one's ability to understand the other in more complex ways."[23]

RELIGIOUS CREOLES: THE CREOLIZATION OF
ELIYAHU MCLEAN

Rabbi Marc Gopin's study of peacemakers in the Middle East narrates how the religious adaptation that Mohammed Abu-Nimer envisions and proposes is possible. Gopin has examined many of the exemplars of such competence—religious "Creoles"—in the Holy Land in *Bridges across an Impossible Divide: The Inner Lives of Arab and Jewish Peacemakers*.[24]

The central figure in Gopin's study supporting Abu-Nimer's proposition that religious adaptation is possible is Eliyahu McLean. I met Eliyahu while visiting Jerusalem in 2006. I had read about him in *At the Entrance to the Garden of Eden* by Israeli journalist Yossi Klein Halevi.[25] This book tells about Halevi's personal spiritual project to meet his Muslim and Christian neighbors in the Holy Land by joining with them in their worship spaces. Eliyahu was his guide, especially into Islamic spaces. Eliyahu McLean is Jewish and has been building interfaith relationships for over twenty-five years. He has developed a wide range of relationships among Muslims, Jews, Christians, and Druze, including very conservative Muslims and Jews who normally eschew interreligious friendship. One method he used was to invite people of diverse religions to his home to celebrate the various religious holidays with an interfaith group.[26] Out of this relational web emerged the Jerusalem Peacemakers network.

Raised in Hawaii, Eliyahu McLean visited Israel for the first time at age fifteen. After graduation from high school he moved to Israel and lived in a Galilean kibbutz for a year. He returned to the United States to study as an undergraduate at Berkeley. He was a pro-Israel activist but encountered pro-Palestinian activists and discovered another narrative. This engagement prompted him to study the Arabic language, the religion of Islam, and Middle Eastern studies. He returned to Israel for his junior year of college to study at Hebrew University in Jerusalem. He met a Palestinian student from the Deheishe Refugee Camp who was studying at Bethlehem University and began hosting Berkeley students in Bethlehem. Eliyahu reflects, "That was the beginning of my bridge building work."[27] We now examine the journey of Eliyahu McLean (and a few of his colleagues) through the lens of creolization. More specifically we consider religious creolization as a response to oppression that restores identity and engenders self-acceptance, heals and humanizes individuals and communities, and revolutionizes societies.

Immersion into Islam with Identity Rooted in Judaism

Eliyahu McLean's immersion into Arab communities and the religion of Islam accelerated when his academic program at Hebrew University was cancelled due to the Gulf War, and he needed to get a job. He found a job as a construction worker. Eliyahu describes the situation: "I was living on the construction site with Palestinian construction workers from Hebron, including [Sufi] sheiks [religious Muslim teachers] from Hebron who were there as construction workers."[28] He learned the spoken Palestinian dialect of Arabic and developed relationships with Palestinian construction workers. After work, Eliyahu would go for evening study at an Orthodox Jewish study center, called a yeshiva, in the Jewish Quarter of the Old City in Jerusalem. Eliyahu was living culturally and to some degree religiously in two worlds. He describes an encounter that illustrated this reality.

> I had a friend, a Palestinian friend from the construction site. This was now 1990–91, and [I also had] a Jewish friend I had been studying with years before who had become a *Ba'al Teshuva* [a Jewish convert to Orthodox Judaism]. He had returned to Judaism, now wearing black hat, black coat [symbols of ultra-Orthodox Judaism]. And they both said hello to me at the same moment. And in Arabic and in Hebrew, *Ken, Aiwa*, I said to them (that is I said to both simultaneously in Hebrew and English, "yes"). And they looked at each other almost in horror, "How does he know *that* guy?" And that was a realization in a moment that I was walking in different worlds.[29]

Eliyahu used the money he earned in construction to travel to Egypt, where he became more fluent in Arabic and more deeply involved in Islamic contexts. He states, "It was in Cairo that I met a West African Sufi who became my *hevruta*, my spiritual study partner."[30] Rabbi Marc Gopin notes that *hevruta* is a singularly Jewish Aramaic Talmudic term. Yet Eliyahu uses it to define his spiritual study partnership with a West African Sufi Muslim. For Gopin, "labeling a Muslim as a *hevruta* embodies the bold act of boundary crossing."[31] Eliyahu describes this relationship with his Sufi Muslim study partner:

> Through that process I went deep into a study of Islam and Sufism in Egypt. And so when I came back to Israel two months later I felt like I had a much deeper connection with Islam and Arabic and Islamic spirituality. From that moment forward, I could relate to religious Muslims and sheikhs and people of faith from the Islamic community. . . . I went into a period, you have to understand, of prayer in the Islamic tradition, learning from the inside about their realm. And till this day, when I speak to the most simple Palestinian, [or] to the most high-level sheikh, they automatically feel a bond with me, even beyond words.

Eliyahu reflects on the effects of this deep immersion experience into Islam and its religio-cultural ways.

> That time that I had in the Old City working construction work, and shortly after in Egypt with the Sufis in Egypt, was a seminal life experience for me that informs me to this day. [It] has given me a tool to know how to reach out, on the one hand, to the religious Jewish community, because I

was studying in yeshiva in the Old City [of Jerusalem] in a very right wing
religious context, and also went into a deep study of Islam in Egypt.[32]

Clearly, Eliyahu's deep immersion into Islam while maintaining an
anchor in his own Judaism caused a shift in his understanding of his
identity. Marc Gopin defines Eliyahu's identity as a bridge identity or "a
mystical union of identities."[33] For Eliyahu, the secret is staying rooted
in his Jewish identity while acquiring an Islamic frame of reference. "I
am not giving up my Jewish heritage or trying to cut off my roots. . . . I
am proud that I was able to move to Israel and make (*Aliyah*). So I have
all the cards to have legitimacy within the Jewish community. So then
I can bring in my more right wing and skeptical . . . circle of friends to
a space to be able to meet the Palestinians on the other side."[34] Eliyahu
continues:

> It is important for me to be firmly grounded within my own close circle of
> friends on the Israeli side and also on the religious Jewish side. [I do this in
> order to] not negate and not to nullify my Jewishness. . . . In order to make
> an impact I have to stay and keep wearing my *payos* [Hasidic Jewish side
> curls] and keep wearing my *tzitzit* [traditional Jewish fringes on garments]
> and stay as someone who is fully connected to that community.[35]

Healing through Interfaith Partnership

For Eliyahu McLean, partnerships and friendships are the path to healing
and reconciliation in the Holy Land. His web of connections spans the
entire extent of the Holy Land including Palestinians living in Israel,
the West Bank, and Gaza. Through these relationships with Arab and
Palestinian Muslims and Christians, he serves as a link of reconciliation
to Jews. "I can then call on those friends to bring *their* friends and *their*
network of friends. And before you know it you have a cascading effect
where thousands of Palestinians know that there are religious Jews who
grew up in Zionist movements like me, who now want to build a bridge
of peace."[36]

Eliyahu also serves as a bridge for Jews to discover relationships with
people of other religions. He reflects, "We want to connect as human
beings, but we have so many walls of fear, walls of fear between us and
the other. But our friend Eliyahu has broken through that wall. . . .
Maybe he can lead the way and show us how it's possible, how it can be
done."[37] Eliyahu's Creole-like journey through secular Zionist activism,
yeshiva, speaking Arabic, ongoing immersion in Palestinian communities, and study and practice of Islam has made him an instrument of heal-

ing. Eliyahu believes this has occurred by "knowing how to express ideas and concepts to build a bridge within [others'] worldview."[38] Eliyahu is expressing what Mohammed Abu-Nimer calls religious adaptation. Eliyahu is a religious Creole.

Eventually Eliyahu looked for a primary partner in his healing work, another Creole-like person with similar adaptation abilities. Due to his previous connection with the Sufi sheikh in Egypt, he was looking for a Sufi partner. A partnership and friendship of this kind could expand the possibilities for peace and healing. Eliyahu found such a partner in the late Sheikh Abdul Aziz Bukhari.[39] I met Sheikh Bukhari in 2007. I visited his home in the Old City of Jerusalem on the Via Dolorosa near the Al Aqsa Mosque and the Haram al-Sharif. His family has lived in the same house since 1616. He was the head of the Naqshabandi Sufi order in Jerusalem, a leading Muslim voice for peace, and a direct descendent of Imam Bukhari—an Islamic scholar renowned for his collecting and writing down the Hadith, that is the commentary of the prophet Muhammad.

Their partnership formed when both were at a conference in Uzbekistan and were invited to pray at the tomb of Imam Bukhari. Eliyahu says, "Underneath the ground there is a special door and very rarely are people allowed there. But because he is a descendant of Imam Bukhari we are allowed there. . . . We both felt then, looking back, that it felt like Imam Bukhari himself gave us his blessing."[40] Sheikh Bukhari adds, "We went to the tomb of Imam Bukhari, and we did prayer over there. And I think—that's my feeling but I think it's true—the Imam Bukhari blessed us and he binded us, because after we came back we started working together."[41] Eliyahu describes the power and impact of their partnership:

> The most fundamental thing is when I'm able to bring right wing skeptics, friends who have never met an Arab, a Muslim, a Palestinian, and bring the sheikh to my house for Shabbat [Sabbath] dinner, or to bring them into his center in the Old City. . . . Sheikh Bukhari in a certain way is a portal way for many Israeli people who have never met a Muslim and a religious Muslim. . . . They see by the love and friendship that we have between us an example on a small scale of the peace we are talking about and trying to manifest on a large scale.[42]

I first experienced their partnership in 2007 when I spent a day with Eliyahu and Sheikh Bukhari at a conference in Netanya, Israel, called "Third Party Involvement in the Peace Process."[43] Then–vice prime minister of Israel Shimon Peres was the keynote speaker. Eliyahu was dressed as an Orthodox Jew, and Sheikh Bukhari was in his Muslim religious garb. We arrived late and burst into the room as Shimon Peres was giving his keynote address. All eyes turned in the direction of these Jerusalem Peacemakers. Throughout the rest of the day, they were the center of attention. What I saw in action was the enactment of a public parable of reconciliation and healing. Eliyahu and Sheikh Bukhari visually communicated the possibility that friendship can exist across the lines of religion and culture. Their friendship and partnership also foreshadowed a new and revolutionary way of living. They were building a network of relationships, across the boundaries of religion, for when peace comes to the Holy Land.

Revolution through Relationships

On that same visit to the Holy Land in 2007, Eliyahu McLean, Sheikh Bukhari, and I travelled to the Orthodox Jewish outpost settlement of Tekoa deep in the West Bank, which is the ancestral home of the biblical prophet Amos.[44] Palestinians consider the construction of these settlements not only illegal and unjust but an insult to their human dignity. The Zionist Orthodox Jews who construct and dwell in outpost settlements like Tekoa believe that God gave them this land, and they are simply reclaiming land promised to them. There were tensions between Israeli Jews in Tekoa and neighboring Palestinian Arabs in the much older village of Teqoa (Tuqu'). Upon arrival in Tekoa, Eliyahu and I left Sheikh Bukhari at the car while we viewed a picturesque canyon at Tekoa called by local Palestinians Wadi Khareitoun (Khreiton). When we returned, four young men from the town were pointing automatic weapons at the sheikh, who was still in the car. He said that they had been interrogating him. Speaking in Hebrew, Eliyahu informed the young vigilantes that we were in town to visit their rabbi. This eased the tensions a bit. The late Rabbi Menachem Froman (d. 2013) was the highly revered and respected rabbi in Tekoa, internationally known for his peacemaking efforts and a member of the Jerusalem Peacemakers.

Shortly thereafter we were stopped by an Israeli police officer who questioned us and pointed at Sheikh Bukhari, saying he was the problem. Then he switched to Hebrew and spoke at some length about why Arabs were a problem for Israel. When the police officer paused for a moment, Eliyahu shared with him that we were on a mission of peace among people of different religions. We were traveling together as a Jew, a Muslim, and a Christian. Unexpectedly the officer toned down his bravado and recounted that he had migrated to Israel from Chile, where people of many religions lived side by side. Instantly and simultaneously both

Eliyahu and Sheikh Bukhari exclaimed, "*¡Hola! ¿Cómo estás?*" The officer began to laugh, and he released us. Our traveling together as an inter-faith team disrupted the status quo of religious separation. It was a revo-lutionary act in the outpost settlement of Tekoa.

Next, we went to the rabbi's yeshiva. The Arab Sheikh Bukhari spoke in flawless Hebrew to the young students of Judaism, teaching them about his Islamic Sufism. We enjoyed a brief glimpse of religious adapta-tion and creolization as he communicated elements of his Islamic faith in Hebrew in a yeshiva. Finally, we found Rabbi Menachem Froman at his home. Froman was an unusual Orthodox settler rabbi. He was a founder of the Gush Emunim messianic settler movement and a rabbi in the out-post settlement of Tekoa. Yet he was "Israel's leading and virtually lone proponent of dialogue with Islam."[45] His activism for peace was inspired by the Scriptures and his love for God. Rabbi Froman had close relation-ships with many Palestinians, both Muslims and Christians. When we arrived, Froman was preparing to lead evening prayers. With his long, white beard, the rabbi looked like a modern-day Amos in Tekoa. He greeted Eliyahu and me, but he repeatedly hugged Sufi Muslim Sheikh Bukhari, saying affectionately that when he lost track of time, the Mus-lim call to prayer would always remind him that it was time for him to pray also.

Rabbi Froman's passion for peace led him to form relationships with the late Palestinian political and liberation leader Yasser Arafat and with the late Sheikh Ahmed Yassin, the spiritual founder of Hamas (who was assassinated by an Israeli helicopter missile strike on his car as he left a mosque in Gaza). Yossi Klein Halevi describes an encounter between Rabbi Froman and Sheikh Yassin that illustrates an interfaith revolution-ary in action:

> When Yassin was released from prison, Froman traveled to the sheykh's home in Gaza and was photographed greeting him while wearing tefillin, extending a hand of peace bound in the straps of Jewish devotion. Yassin invited him onto the stage of his welcome-home rally, and the settler rabbi, embodiment of the Zionist enemy, calmly faced thousands of Hamas sup-porters chanting death slogans aimed at his people. . . . He was ready to talk to any Muslim, under any circumstances, to help transform religion from a pretext for hatred into an instrument for healing. . . . If the Jews had been replanted in the biblical land, just as the prophets had predicted, then surely the prophets' vision of peace between Israel and the nations was also within reach. And the most urgent place to begin was healing the ancient feud between Isaac and Ishmael.[46]

Marc Gopin writes that what Rabbi Froman envisioned "was nothing less than revolutionary." Gopin declares that his plan was for "a first-time-ever treaty or covenant between Judaism and Islam. In particular, they hoped that the public events surrounding this, and the accompanying symbolism, such as the jolting effect of chief rabbis and sheikhs embracing, would create a religious-psychological breakthrough that would generate its own momentum of peacemaking."[47]

Eliyahu McLean, Sheikh Bukhari, and Rabbi Froman resolved to revolutionize society through risky interfaith relationships. They each believed that their Abrahamic belief in one God—the same God—made this possible. This is nowhere more apparent than in a 2008 interview with the Global Oneness Project, where Rabbi Froman recounted a conversation he had with Hamas founder Sheikh Yassin regarding religion and peace. Sheikh Yassin said to Rabbi Froman, "You and I could make peace in five minutes. Why? Because we are both religious. Is there any doubt concerning who rules this land? We both know who rules this land, who is the Master." Pointing upward toward heaven, Rabbi Froman finished Sheikh Yassin's words, "The Master of the Universe."[48] Froman saw interfaith relationships in the Holy Land as acts of revolution!

Yossi Klein Halevi tells of a most dramatic moment with Eliyahu McLean that reveals the power of his revolutionary relational reconciliation. Eliyahu wanted to visit Sheikh Abdul-Rahim in the Gaza Strip. He was the spiritual head of the Rifa`i Sufi order in Palestine. Halevi explains why Eliyahu so fervently wanted to visit the "sheikh of sheykhs." He writes, "It was no simple matter for a sheykh, even a Sufi, to host a Jew in a Gaza mosque. . . . Ecumenical contacts with Islam became increasingly difficult the deeper you penetrated the Palestinian tragedy: Dialogue was possible with Palestinian citizens of Israel, rare with West Bank Palestinians, and, with Gaza refugees, almost inconceivable."[49] Eliyahu believed that a meeting with Sheikh Abdul-Rahim would lead to an introduction to Gaza's Muslim community. So Eliyahu and Yossi Halevi were invited to participate in prayers in the Gazan sheikh's mosque in the Nuseirat refugee camp. Halevi tells the story:

> We're sitting with the sheikh and his people, and the sheikh is repeatedly trying to convert us. And every time Eliyahu or I engage him in a question or try to engage him in dialogue his response is "if you don't love the prophet Muhammad then you can't love me." And of course we are trying to say to him we come with great reverence, with great love for the prophet Muhammad, for Islam, but we're Jews and we're not looking to change our religion.

Halevi whispered to Eliyahu that the situation was hopeless and they should depart. Then suddenly Eliyahu asks the sheikh to take them to the tomb. Sheikh Abdul-Rahim had told them that the mosque had been intentionally built next to the tomb of his holy and beloved sheikh. Sheikh Abdul-Rahim grabs Eliyahu's hand, and they go to the tomb and enter it. Halevi shares, "The sheikh is explaining to us who his teacher was, and how in the presence of death . . . all of human vanity disappears." When they return to the mosque the sheikh's attitude was transformed. Halevi sums up what happened:

> Eliyahu had understood, somehow intuitively, that the way to break through this theological impasse was to reach the point where the sheikh's devotion was centered, and the sheikh's devotion was centered in the love for his sheikh and in the sense that before death, when you stand before death, all of human differences, all of our human ideas fall away. And the sheikh was a different person after he took us into the tomb. . . . He said, "Ever since I held your hand and you held my hand inside of the tomb you've been one of mine." . . . Eliyahu had found the way into the sheikh's heart.[50]

Eliyahu's interreligious competence enabled him to shift his religious frame of reference and understand the heart of the sheikh. And he switched his behavior and words to an Islamic stance. This Creole-like action opened a sacred space for reconciliation.

During my 2007 visit to Tekoa with Eliyahu and Sheikh Bukhari, I gave Rabbi Froman a copy of my book *Reconciliation*.[51] As he looked at the book, he told an old story from the rabbis. It seems that someone asked God what the divine had been doing since finishing work on the sixth day of creation. God replied that the Almighty's post-creation work was matching people, in other words, reconciliation. Rabbi Froman added that as followers of God our work should also be reconciliation, because reconciliation is our greatest act of worship. A few years later, Sheikh Ghassan Manasra, another Sufi member of the Jerusalem Peacemakers, joined Eliyahu in lecturing for a course I taught at Bethel University. He told this story:

> A Sufi sheikh and his disciple were walking. The disciple, describing a conflict with a fellow disciple, asked the Sufi for his wisdom. The Sufi sheikh asked, "Do you want the truth or something greater than the truth?" The disciple replied, "I have come to you on a search for truth and now you tell me there is something greater than truth. What is greater than truth?" The Sufi said, "Reconciliation."[52]

Eliyahu McLean, Sheikh Aziz Abdul Bukhari, Rabbi Menachem Froman, and Sheikh Ghassan Manasra—all Jerusalem Peacemakers—"cognitively, morally, and emotionally chose to live in . . . radically different worlds."[53] Living in multiple religious worlds creolizes people of faith to revolutionize society. As modern-day Ishmaels and Isaacs (and Hagars and Sarahs), we can choose to be reconciled at the cave of Machpelah.

Notes

1. The story of Abraham's burial is found only in the first book of the Hebrew Scriptures. The Qur'an does not tell of Abraham's death. Both Ishmael and Isaac are honored as prophets in the Qur'an.

2. The tomb of Abraham and Sarah is presently in the West Bank of the Occupied Palestinian Territories. The tomb is highly contested between Jews and Muslims in the Holy Land and has witnessed tragic violence. Therefore, there are separate entrances into the tomb for each group.

3. Marc Gopin, *Holy War, Holy Peace: How Religion Can Bring Peace to the Middle East* (New York: Oxford University Press, 2002), 54–55.

4. Jonathan Morgan and Steven J. Sandage, "A Developmental Model of Interreligious Competence: A Conceptual Framework," *Archive for the Psychology of Religion* 38 (2016): 138.

5. Mohammed Abu-Nimer, "Conflict Resolution, Culture, and Religion: Toward a Training Model of Interreligious Peacebuilding," *Journal of Peace Research* 38, no. 6 (2001): 700.

6. Mohammed Abu-Nimer, Amal I. Khoury, and Emily Welty, *Unity in Diversity: Interfaith Dialogue in the Middle East* (Washington, DC: United States Institute of Peace, 2007), 33.

7. Abu-Nimer, "Conflict Resolution, Culture, and Religion," 700.

8. Abu-Nimer, "Conflict Resolution, Culture, and Religion," 701.

9. Hizkias Assefa, "Coexistence and Reconciliation in the Northern Region of Ghana," in *Reconciliation, Justice, and Coexistence: Theory and Practice*, ed. Mohammed Abu-Nimer (Lanham, MD: Lexington, 2001), 184–85.

10. Mohammed Abu-Nimer, "Religion, Dialogue, and Non-Violent Actions in Palestinian-Israeli Conflict," *International Journal of Politics, Culture, and Society* 17, no. 3 (Spring 2004): 491–511.

11. Abu-Nimer, "Religion, Dialogue, and Non-Violent Actions," 502.

12. Darrell J. Fasching and Dell Dechant, *Comparative Religious Ethics: A Narrative Approach* (Oxford: Blackwell, 2001), 156.

13. Mohammed Abu-Nimer, "The Miracles of Transformation through Inter-faith Dialogue: Are You a Believer?," in *Interfaith Dialogue and Peace Building*, ed. David R. Smock (Washington, DC: United States Institute of Peace, 2002), 18.

14. Abu-Nimer, "Religion, Dialogue, and Non-Violent Actions," 503, 505.

15. Morgan and Sandage, "Developmental Model of Interreligious Competence," 146–47.

16. Morgan and Sandage, "Developmental Model of Interreligious Competence," 146–47, quoting Thomas Merton, "Monastic Experience and the East-West Dialogue," in *The World Religions Speak on "The Relevance of Religion in the Modern World,"* ed. F. P. Dunne (Netherlands: Springer, 1970), 73.

17. Morgan and Sandage, "Developmental Model of Interreligious Competence," 147.

18. Morgan and Sandage, "Developmental Model of Interreligious Competence," 147. See also Howard Thurman, *The Search for Common Ground: An Inquiry into the Basis of Man's Experience of Community* (New York: Harper & Row, 1971).

19. Seyyed Hossein Nasr, "What Attracted Merton to Sufism," in *Merton & Sufism: The Untold Story*, ed. Rob Baker and Gray Henry (Louisville: Fons Vitae, 1999), 9.

20. Howard Thurman, *A Strange Freedom: The Best of Howard Thurman on Religious Experience*, ed. Walter Earl Fluker and Catherine Tumer (Boston: Beacon, 1998), 109.

21. I observed this happen at a Christian university where Mohammed Abu-Nimer was presenting on his religion-adapted DMIS. Most of the faculty and staff were supportive of his research when it spoke generally of culture. But when he began to discuss religious adaptation, the audience was very uncomfortable and resistant.

22. Abu-Nimer et al., *Unity in Diversity*, 34–35.

23. Abu-Nimer et al., *Unity in Diversity*, 28.

24. Marc Gopin, *Bridges across an Impossible Divide: The Inner Lives of Arab and Jewish Peacemakers* (New York: Oxford University Press, 2012).

25. Yossi Klein Halevi, *At the Entrance to the Garden of Eden: A Jew's Search for Hope with Christians and Muslims in the Holy Land* (New York: Perennial, 2002).

26. Gopin, *Bridges across an Impossible Divide*, 47.

27. Gopin, *Bridges across an Impossible Divide*, 49.

28. Gopin, *Bridges across an Impossible Divide*, 51.

29. Gopin, *Bridges across an Impossible Divide*, 51–52.

30. Gopin, *Bridges across an Impossible Divide*, 53.

31. Gopin, *Bridges across an Impossible Divide*, 54.

32. Gopin, *Bridges across an Impossible Divide*, 54–55.

33. Gopin, *Bridges across an Impossible Divide*, 55.

34. Gopin, *Bridges across an Impossible Divide*, 57–58.

35. Gopin, *Bridges across an Impossible Divide*, 59.

36. Gopin, *Bridges across an Impossible Divide*, 57.

37. Gopin, *Bridges across an Impossible Divide*, 59.

38. Gopin, *Bridges across an Impossible Divide*, 62.

39. Sheikh Bukhari died in 2010. Gopin notes that the chapter written in his book "is the only chapter ever written in Sheikh Bukhari's own words." See Gopin, *Bridges across an Impossible Divide*, 79–100.

40. Gopin, *Bridges across an Impossible Divide*, 67.

41. Gopin, *Bridges across an Impossible Divide*, 83.

42. Gopin, *Bridges across an Impossible Divide*, 73. See the video by Zej Media, "Unusual Pairs: Eliyahu McLean and Sheikh Aziz Abdul Bukhari," September 15, 2009, https://tinyurl.com/y93lgtb2.

43. Curtiss Paul DeYoung, *Homecoming: A "White" Man's Journey through Harlem to Jerusalem* (Eugene, OR: Wipf & Stock, 2015), 123–24.

44. DeYoung, *Homecoming*, 124–26.

45. Halevi, *At the Entrance to the Garden of Eden*, 87.

46. Halevi, *At the Entrance to the Garden of Eden*, 88.

47. Gopin, *Holy War, Holy Peace*, 45.

48. For interview with Rabbi Menachem Froman, see his profile at the Global Oneness Project: https://tinyurl.com/k5oyp8d.

49. Halevi, *At the Entrance to the Garden of Eden*, 269.

50. Gopin, *Bridges across an Impossible Divide*, 74–75.

51. Curtiss Paul DeYoung, *Reconciliation: Our Greatest Challenge; Our Only Hope* (Valley Forge, PA: Judson, 1997).

52. Ghassan Manasra, speaking with Eliyahu McLean, "Reconcilers in the Holy Land," Bethel University, St. Paul, Minnesota, November 14, 2011.

53. Gopin, *Bridges across an Impossible Divide*, 52.

Postlude

CURTISS PAUL DEYOUNG

In Revelation, the final book of the New Testament, the mystic author describes what he saw in an apocalyptic vision while on the Isle of Patmos. It is the second half of the first century, and the oppressive and violent colonial power of the Roman Empire is in full sway. The author, John, is an oppressed Jew writing as one who has been transformed by the Creole-like formation process of the first-century Pentecost church. There is a moment when he records an image he sees in his vision: "After this I looked, and there was a great multitude that no one could count, from every nation, from all tribes and peoples and languages, standing before . . . God who is seated on the throne" (Rev 7:9–10). Amid Roman oppression and colonization, he is shown a vision of a future that is fully inclusive and encompasses every nation, all tribes, all peoples, and all languages. There is no power hierarchy evident, except for God on the throne. John the Revelator proclaims God's vision of a Creole-like future.

From the Isle of Martinique, Jean Bernabé, Patrick Chamoiseau, and Raphaël Confiant, the authors of *Éloge de la Créolité / In Praise of Creoleness*, describe their future global vision of Creole cultural identity. Their vision resonates with that seen by John the Revelator on the Isle of Patmos in the first century. They write,

> A new humanity will gradually emerge which will have the same characteristics as our Creole humanity: all the complexity of Creoleness. The son or daughter of a German and a Haitian, born and living in Peking, will be torn between several languages, several histories, caught in the torrential ambiguity of a mosaic identity. To present creative depth, one must perceive that identity in all its complexity. He or she will be in the situation of a Creole.[1]

Emerging out of a history of colonization and slavery, they envision a Creole future that stands in contrast with current global realities.

Hope for a future like that proclaimed by John the Revelator and the Creole authors of *Éloge de la Créolité*—free from oppression and injustice, when a new humanity includes all peoples, languages, tribes, and nations—now exists in the realm of mystery. Only the mystics see and experience it in its fullness. As individuals and as communities of faith enter into a process of creolization, we will begin to see in earthly formation glimpses of this Creole mystery. And we will be, more and more, in the situation of a Creole.

Notes

1. Jean Bernabé, Patrick Chamoiseau, and Raphaël Confiant, *Éloge de la Créolité / In Praise of Creoleness*, Édition Bilingue (Paris: Gallimard, 1993), 112.

Acknowledgments

CURTISS PAUL DEYOUNG

This book was nearly ten years in the making. It was birthed on the Isle of Guadeloupe and proceeded through various job transitions: I began researching as a professor of reconciliation studies at Bethel University living in Minneapolis; I organized and proposed the book after moving to Chicago as the executive director of Community Renewal Society; and I finished writing back in Minneapolis as the CEO of the Minnesota Council of Churches. The book process gained some momentum while I was homebound and slowed down while recovering from surgery on a torn Achilles tendon. I found inspiration while writing at many different beaches—at oceans and Lake Michigan. The beach scenario somehow seems appropriate for a book discussing French Caribbean Creole.

I express much gratitude to the contributing authors of this book: Jacqui Lewis, Micky ScottBey Jones, Robyn Afrik, Sarah Thompson Nahar, Sindy Morales Garcia, and 'Iwalani Ka'ai. Each is an inspiration to me and a gift to this book. I have journeyed with Jacqui and Robyn for many years as valued colleagues and close friends. Sindy and 'Iwalani were my students and teaching assistants—now friends and writing partners. I met Micky and Sarah in the past few years in the context of activism. I met Micky in Ferguson, Missouri, and Sarah with Palestinian activists. My very first conversations with both of them in those settings included some of the stories now in this book.

Special thanks to Scott Tunseth and Beth Gaede from Fortress Press. This is my fourth project with Fortress. Additional thanks to Sarah Thompson Nahar for some inspired editing. I was honored to speak about my musings with Dr. Ruby Sales in what was a spiritually enlightening phone conversation. Much appreciation to Suzi Nelson and Jonathan DeYoung, who typed sections of my research. My dear friends Cecilia Williams and Robin Bell have been a source of consistent encouragement in the writing of this book. And much love to my family—Karen, Rachel, Jonathan, and Dane. All praise to the God of Abraham, Sarah, and Hagar, to Jesus, and to the Spirit of Pentecost.

Bibliography

Abrahams, Roger D. "About Face: Rethinking Creolization." In *Creolization as Cultural Creativity*, edited by Robert Baron and Ana C. Cara, 285–305. Jackson: University Press of Mississippi, 2011.

Abu-Nimer, Mohammed. "Conflict Resolution, Culture, and Religion: Toward a Training Model of Interreligious Peacebuilding." *Journal of Peace Research* 38, no. 6 (2001): 685–704.

———. "The Miracles of Transformation through Interfaith Dialogue: Are You a Believer?" In *Interfaith Dialogue and Peace Building*, edited by David R. Smock, 15–32. Washington, DC: United States Institute of Peace, 2002.

———. "Religion, Dialogue, and Non-Violent Actions in Palestinian-Israeli Conflict." *International Journal of Politics, Culture, and Society* 17, no. 3 (Spring 2004): 491–511.

Abu-Nimer, Mohammed, Amal I. Khoury, and Emily Welty. *Unity in Diversity: Interfaith Dialogue in the Middle East.* Washington, DC: United States Institute of Peace, 2007.

Adler, Peter S. "Beyond Cultural Identity: Reflections on Multiculturalism." In *Basic Concepts of Intercultural Communication*, edited by Milton J. Bennett, 224–45. Boston: Intercultural Press, 1998.

Applegate, Beth. "My Journey Is a Slow, Steady Awakening." In *Embracing Cultural Competency: A Roadmap for Nonprofit Capacity Builders*, lead author Patricia St. Onge, 17–30. Saint Paul: Fieldstone Alliance, 2009.

Assefa, Hizkias. "Coexistence and Reconciliation in the Northern Region of Ghana." In *Reconciliation, Justice, and Coexistence: Theory and Practice,* edited by Mohammed Abu-Nimer, 165–86. Lanham, MD: Lexington, 2001.

Baldwin, James. *The Fire Next Time.* New York: Vintage International, 1993.

Balutansky, Kathleen M., and Marie-Agnès Sourieau. Introduction to *Caribbean Creolization: Reflections on the Cultural Dynamics of Language, Literature, and Identity,* edited by Kathleen M. Balutansky and Marie-Agnès Sourieau, 1–11. Gainesville: University Press of Florida, 1998.

———. "Part One: Creolization and the Creative Imagination." In *Caribbean Creolization: Reflections on the Cultural Dynamics of Language, Literature, and Identity,* edited by Kathleen M. Balutansky and Marie-Agnès Sourieau, 21–22. Gainesville: University Press of Florida, 1998.

Baron, Robert, and Ana C. Cara. "Introduction: Creolization as Cultural Creativity." In *Creolization as Cultural Creativity,* edited by Robert Baron and Ana C. Cara, 3–19. Jackson: University Press of Mississippi, 2011.

Beasley-Murray, George R. *Word Biblical Commentary.* Volume 36. Waco: Word, 1987.

Bender, Steven W. *One Night in America: Robert Kennedy, César Chávez, and the Dream of Dignity.* Boulder: Paradigm, 2008.

Bennett, Janet M., and Milton J. Bennett. "Developing Intercultural Sensitivity: An Integrative Approach to Global and Domestic Diversity." In *Handbook of Intercultural Training,* 3rd ed., edited by Dan Landis, Janet M. Bennett, and Milton J. Bennett, 147–65. Thousand Oaks, CA: SAGE, 2004.

Bennett, Milton J. "Intercultural Communication: A Current Perspective." In *Basic Concepts of Intercultural Communication,* edited by Milton J. Bennett, 1–34. Boston: Intercultural Press, 1998.

Bernabé, Jean, Patrick Chamoiseau, and Raphaël Confiant. *Éloge de la Créolité / In Praise of Creoleness.* Édition Bilingue. Paris: Gallimard, 1993.

Blake, John. "When You Are the Only White Person in the Room." CNN.com. September 11, 2014. https://tinyurl.com/yc2pncqn.

Boesak, Allan Aubrey, and Curtiss Paul DeYoung. *Radical Reconciliation: Beyond Political Pietism and Christian Quietism.* Maryknoll, NY: Orbis, 2012.

Bohrer, John R. *The Revolution of Robert Kennedy: From Power to Protest after JFK.* New York: Bloomsbury, 2017.

Boyd, Drick. *White Allies in the Struggle for Racial Justice.* Maryknoll, NY: Orbis, 2015.

Caldwell, Roy Chandler, Jr.. "Créolité and Postcoloniality in Raphaël Confiant's L'Allées des Soupirs." *The French Review* 73, no. 2 (Dec. 1999): 301–11.

Césaire, Aimé. *Discourse on Colonialism.* Rev. ed. New York: Monthly Review, 2000.

Chamoiseau, Patrick, Raphaël Confiant, Jean Bernabé, and Lucien Taylor. "Créolité Bites: A Conversation with Patrick Chamoiseau, Raphaël Confiant, and Jean Bernabé." *Transition* 74 (1997): 124–61.

Clancy, Frank. "The Reconciler." *Minnesota Monthly,* June 2004, 56–61.

Clarke, Thurston. *The Last Campaign: Robert F. Kennedy and 82 Days That Inspired America.* New York: Henry Holt and Company, 2008.

Coates, Ta-Nehisi. *Between the World and Me*. New York: Spiegl & Grau, 2015.

Cohen, Robin, and Paola Toninato. "The Creolization Debate: Analyzing Mixed Identities and Cultures." In *The Creolization Reader: Studies in Mixed Identities and Cultures*, edited by Robin Cohen and Paola Toninato, 1–21. London: Routledge, 2010.

Crossan, John Dominic, and Jonathan L. Reed. *In Search of Paul: How Jesus's Apostle Opposed Rome's Empire with God's Kingdom*. San Francisco: HarperSanFrancisco, 2004.

deGregory, Crystal A. "HBCUs Ain't Handing Out Black Cards: Howard's Rachel Dolezal + Faux-Blackness." *hbcustory*, June 13, 2015. https://tinyurl.com/y79aqc9z.

DeYoung, Curtiss Paul. *Coming Together in the 21st Century: The Bible's Message in an Age of Diversity*. Valley Forge, PA: Judson, 2009.

———. *Homecoming: A "White" Man's Journey through Harlem to Jerusalem*. Eugene, OR: Wipf & Stock, 2015.

———. *Living Faith: How Faith Inspires Social Justice*. Minneapolis: Fortress, 2007.

———. *Mystiques en action: Trois modèles pour le XXIe siècle: Dietrich Bonhoeffer, Malcolm X, Aung San Suu Kyi*. Genève, Switzerland: Labor et fides, 2010.

———. "Racial Equity and Faith-Based Organizing at Community Renewal Society." In *Urban Ministry Reconsidered: Contexts and Approaches*, edited by R. Drew Smith, Stephanie C. Boddie, and Ronald E. Peters, 89–96. Louisville: Westminster John Knox, 2018.

———. *Reconciliation: Our Greatest Challenge—Our Only Hope*. Valley Forge, PA: Judson, 1997.

DiAngelo, Robin. *What Does It Mean to Be White? Developing White Racial Literacy*. Rev. ed. New York: Peter Lang, 2016.

Doležal, Rachel. *In Full Color: Finding My Place in a Black and White World*. Dallas: BenBella, 2017.

Du Bois, W. E. B. *The Souls of Black Folk*. Chicago: A. C. McClurg, 1903.

Dyson, Michael Eric. *What Truth Sounds Like: RFK, James Baldwin, and Our Unfinished Conversation about Race in America*. New York: St. Martin's, 2018.

Elliot, Neil. "The Apostle Paul and Empire." In *In the Shadow of Empire: Reclaiming the Bible as a History of Faithful Resistance*, edited by Richard A. Horsley, 97–116. Louisville: Westminster John Knox, 2008.

Emerson, Michael O., and Christian Smith. *Divided by Faith: Evangelical Religion and the Problem of Race in America*. New York: Oxford University Press, 2000.

Endicott, Leilani, Tonia Bock, and Darcia Narvaez. "Moral Reasoning, Inter-cultural Development, and Multicultural Experiences: Relations and Cognitive Underpinnings." *International Journal of Intercultural Relations* 27 (2003): 403–19.

Fanon, Frantz. *Black Skin, White Masks*. New York: Grove, 1967.

Fasching, Darrell J., and Dell Dechant. *Comparative Religious Ethics: A Narrative Approach*. Oxford: Blackwell, 2001.

Felder, Cain Hope. Foreword to *Coming Together: The Bible's Message in an Age of Diversity* by Curtiss Paul DeYoung. Valley Forge, PA: Judson, 1995.

———. *Troubling Biblical Waters: Race, Class, and Family*. Maryknoll, NY: Orbis, 1989.

Finley, Mary Lou, Bernard Lafayette Jr., James R. Ralph Jr., and Pam Smith, eds. *The Chicago Freedom Movement: Martin Luther King Jr. and Civil Rights Activism in the North*. Lexington: University Press of Kentucky, 2016.

Freire, Paulo. *Pedagogy of the Oppressed*. New York: Continuum, 2000.

Gaster, T. H. "Samaritans." In *The Interpreter's Dictionary of the Bible*, vol. 4, edited by George Arthur Buttrick, 190–92. Nashville: Abingdon, 1969.

Glissant, Édouard. *Poetics of Relation*. Ann Arbor: The University of Michigan Press, 1990.

Gopin, Marc. *Bridges across an Impossible Divide: The Inner Lives of Arab and Jewish Peacemakers*. New York: Oxford University Press, 2012.

———. *Holy War, Holy Peace: How Religion Can Bring Peace to the Middle East*. New York: Oxford University Press, 2002.

Halevi, Yossi Klein. *At the Entrance to the Garden of Eden: A Jew's Search for Hope with Christians and Muslims in the Holy Land*. New York: Perennial, 2002.

Hall, Stuart. "Créolité and the Process of Creolization." In *The Creolization Reader: Studies in Mixed Identities and Cultures*, edited by Robin Cohen and Paola Toninato, 26–38. London: Routledge, 2010.

———. "Creolization, Diaspora, and Hybridity in the Context of Globalization." In *Créolité and Creolization*, edited by Okwui Enwezor, Carlos Basualdo, Ute Meta Bauer, Susanne Ghez, Sarat Maharaj, Mark Nash, and Octavio Zaya, 185–98. Ostfildern-Ruit, Germany: Hatje Cantz, 2003.

Hamilton, Edith. *The Greek Way*. New York: W. W. Norton, 1942.

Hammer, Mitchell R. "The Intercultural Development Inventory (IDI): An Approach for Assessing and Building Intercultural Competence." In *Contemporary Leadership and Intercultural Competence: Understanding and Utilizing Cultural Diversity to Build Successful Organizations*, edited by M. A. Moodian, 245–58. Thousand Oaks, CA: SAGE, 2008.

Hammer, Mitchell R., Milton J. Bennett, and Richard Wiseman. "Measuring Intercultural Sensitivity: The Intercultural Development Inventory." *International Journal of Intercultural Relations* 27 (2003): 421–43.

Harris, Wilson. "Creoleness: The Crossroads of a Civilization?" In *Caribbean Creolization: Reflections on the Cultural Dynamics of Language, Literature, and Identity*, edited by Kathleen M. Balutansky and Marie-Agnès Sourieau, 23–35. Gainesville: University Press of Florida, 1998.

Horsley, Richard A. *Jesus and Empire: The Kingdom of God and the New World Order*. Minneapolis: Fortress, 2003.

Horsley, Richard A., and Neil Asher Silverman. *The Message and the Kingdom: How Jesus and Paul Ignited a Revolution and Transformed the Ancient World*. New York: Grosset/Putnam, 1997.

Hughey, Matthew W. "Hegemonic Whiteness: From Structure and Agency to Identity Allegiance." In *The Construction of Whiteness: An Interdisciplinary Analysis of Race Formation and the Meaning of a White Identity*, edited by Stephen Middleton, David R. Roediger, and Donald M. Shaffer, 212–33. Jackson: University Press of Mississippi, 2016.

Jeremias, Joachim. *Jerusalem in the Time of Jesus*. Philadelphia: Fortress, 1969.

Jerkins, Morgan. *This Will Be My Undoing: Living at the Intersection of Black, Female, and Feminist in (White) America*. New York: Harper Perennial, 2018.

Kim, Young Yun. "Beyond Cultural Categories: Communication, Adaptation and Transformation." In *The Routledge Handbook of Language and Intercultural Communication*, edited by Jane Jackson, 229–43. London: Routledge, 2012.

King, Martin Luther, Jr. *I Have a Dream: Writings and Speeches That Changed the World*. Edited by James M. Washington. San Francisco: HarperCollins, 1992.

Lensmire, Timothy J. *White Folks: Race and Identity in Rural America*. New York: Routledge, 2017.

Lewis, Jacqueline J., and John Janka. *The Pentecost Paradigm: 10 Strategies for Becoming a Multiracial Congregation*. Louisville: Westminster John Knox, 2018.

Margolick, David. *The Promise and the Dream: The Untold Story of Martin Luther King, Jr. and Robert F. Kennedy*. New York: Rosetta, 2018.

Michael, Ali. "Rachel Dolezal Syndrome." Educating for Equity (blog). https://tinyurl.com/ps5llrv.

Morgan, Jonathan, and Steven J. Sandage. "A Developmental Model of Interreligious Competence: A Conceptual Framework." *Archive for the Psychology of Religion* 38 (2016): 129–58.

Nasr, Seyyed Hossein. "What Attracted Merton to Sufism." In *Merton & Sufism: The Untold Story*, edited by Rob Baker and Gray Henry, 9–13. Louisville: Fons Vitae, 1999.

Omartian, Stormie. *The Power of a Praying Wife*. Eugene, OR: Harvest House, 1997.

Paige, R. Michael, Melody Jacobs-Cassuto, Yelena A. Yershova, and Joan DeJaeghere. "Assessing Intercultural Sensitivity: An Empirical Analysis of the Hammer and Bennett Intercultural Development Inventory." *International Journal of Intercultural Relations* 27 (2003): 467–86.

Pusch, Margaret D. "The Interculturally Competent Global Leader." In *The SAGE Handbook of Intercultural Competence*, edited by Darla K. Deardorff, 66–84. Los Angeles: SAGE, 2009.

Ralph, James R., Jr. *Northern Protest: Martin Luther King, Jr., Chicago, and the Civil Rights Movement*. Cambridge: Harvard University Press, 1993.

Sidorenko, Konstantin. *Robert F. Kennedy: A Spiritual Biography*. New York: Crossroad, 2000.

Sorrells, Kathryn. *Intercultural Communication: Globalization and Social Justice*. 2nd ed. Los Angeles: SAGE, 2016.

St. Onge, Patricia. Preface to *Embracing Cultural Competency: A Roadmap for Nonprofit Capacity Builders*, lead author Patricia St. Onge, xxiii–xxiv. Saint Paul: Fieldstone Alliance, 2009.

———. "I Can Hear the Heartbeat of the Drum under the Surface of the Words We Speak." In *Embracing Cultural Competency: A Roadmap for Nonprofit Capacity Builders*, lead author Patricia St. Onge, 57–66. Saint Paul: Fieldstone Alliance, 2009.

Suk, Jeannie. *Postcolonial Paradoxes in French Caribbean Writing: Césaire, Glissant, Condé*. New York: Oxford University Press, 2003.

Thomas, Evan. *Robert Kennedy: His Life*. New York: Simon & Schuster, 2000.

Thompson, Becky, and Veronica T. Watson. "Theorizing White Racial Trauma and Its Remedies." In *The Construction of Whiteness: An Interdisciplinary Analysis of Race Formation and the Meaning of a White Identity*, edited by Stephen Middleton, David R. Roediger, and Donald M. Shaffer, 234–55. Jackson: University Press of Mississippi, 2016.

Thurman, Howard. *Disciplines of the Spirit*. New York: Harper & Row, 1963.

———. *The Search for Common Ground: An Inquiry into the Basis of Man's Experience of Community*. New York: Harper & Row, 1971.

———. *A Strange Freedom: The Best of Howard Thurman on Religious Experience*. Edited by Walter Earl Fluker and Catherine Tumer. Boston: Beacon, 1998.

Tutu, Desmond. *No Future without Forgiveness*. New York: Doubleday, 1999.

Vergés, Françoise. "Kiltir Kreol: Processes and Practices of Créolité and Creolization." In *Créolité and Creolization: Documenta11_Platform3*, edited by Okwui Enwezor, Carlos Basualdo, Ute Meta Bauer, Susanne Ghez, Sarat Maharaj, Mark Nash, and Octavio Zaya, 179–84. Ostfildern-Ruit, Germany: Hatje Cantz Publishers, 2003.

Witcover, Jules. *85 Days: The Last Campaign of Robert Kennedy*. New York: William Morrow, 1988.

Contributor Biographies

Robyn Afrik is the founder of Afrik Advantage, an organization dedicated to facilitating honest conversations on how to do inclusion without just talking about it. She's implemented inclusion strategies in the private, public, and nonprofit sectors. Robyn holds a master's in business strategy, management, and leadership from Michigan State University, is a Certified Global Career Development Facilitator (GCDF), and a Certified Cultural Intelligence and Unconscious Bias Facilitator from the Cultural Intelligence Center, and she obtained her board certification from ACG University.

Curtiss Paul DeYoung is the CEO of the Minnesota Council of Churches. Previously he was the executive director of the historic racial justice organization Community Renewal Society in Chicago and the inaugural professor of reconciliation studies at Bethel University in Saint Paul. He earned degrees from the University of St. Thomas, Howard University School of Divinity, and Anderson University. Curtiss is an author and editor of twelve books, including *The Peoples' Bible* and *Living Faith* for Fortress Press.

Micky ScottBey Jones, the Justice Doula, is a womanist-activist-contemplative-healer-holy disrupter who believes in throwing parties as a key revolutionary strategy. She is the director of resilience and healing initiatives with Faith Matters Network and a core team member with The People's Supper (gathering more than four thousand people around tables since the 2016 election for bridging and healing conversations). She is writing a Movement Chaplaincy curriculum and planning more pilgrimages to South Africa. Micky lives in Tennessee with her three brilliant, gorgeous children.

'**Iwalani Ka'ai** is an activist, registered nurse, and lifelong learner-advocate for Native Hawaiian culture, sovereignty, and land rights. She was a board member for the Hawaiian nonprofit 'Ahahui Hawai'i O Minnesota. 'Iwalani was raised by her parents, Jennifer and Harold, in Minnesota before relocating to O'ahu as an adult. She is currently engaged to her fiancé, Ryan, and involved in a Ho'oponopono cohort. 'Iwalani has a degree in nursing and reconciliation studies from Bethel University.

Jacqueline J. Lewis is senior minister at Middle Collegiate Church, a 1,100-member multiracial, welcoming, and inclusive congregation in New York City. She is an activist, preacher, author, and fierce advocate for racial equality, economic justice, and LGBTQIA+ equality. Middle Church and Jacqui's activism for these issues has been featured in media such as *The TODAY Show*, *The Washington Post*, *The New York Times*, *The Wall Street Journal*, *Essence*, and *The Huffington Post*.

Sindy Morales Garcia was born in the mountains of Guatemala and comes from a long line of resilient tricksters and determined community organizers. Driven by a commitment to social justice and wholeness, she works with the Community Initiatives team at the Amherst H. Wilder Foundation in Minnesota. She is a trained facilitator in the Art of Hosting and a Qualified Administrator in the Intercultural Development Inventory. Sindy has degrees from Bethel University, Silberman School of Social Work, and Union Theological Seminary.

Sarah Thompson Nahar is a border-walking scholar-activist from Elkhart, Indiana (traditional Potowatomi land). She focuses her energy in the areas of ecological regeneration, community cultivation, and spiritual activism. She has been a Rotary Peace Fellow, Fulbright Scholar, staff at the Martin Luther King Jr. Center for Nonviolent Social Change, and the executive director of the international organization Christian Peacemaker Teams. Sarah has degrees from Spelman College and Anabaptist Mennonite Biblical Seminary.